Cultivating Meaning
in the Science Classroom
Nurturing Children's Reasoning
THE SCHOOL EXPERIENCE WE ALL WANT

A way of nurturing emotionally strong
interested, interesting human beings

MEREDITH OLSON, Ph.D.

www.DocOsBooks.com

Published by:
SAN 299-2701
Glenhaven Publishing
4262 NE 125 Street
Seattle, Washington 98125

ISBN   978-0-9657061-1-7 (paperback)

Table of Contents

Introduction

A new school year is starting.
The students enter the room.
Silence.
What will it be like?
Expectant but silent.
Students watch me walk to the overhead projector in the center of
their horseshoe of desks.

They tell me my class is strange.
Like no one else.
But they love it here.
They don't want to miss a day of school.
At least not a day of science class.

So, how is it different?
Being a science classroom, there are rules everywhere.
Safety rules.
Protocol rules.
Debating rules. Note - taking, journal rules.
The rules are not written down. They are explained when needed
and just understood.
This is not a democracy. Students do not vote on the rules.
The rules are statements of fact. They are there for a reason.

But why do they love it?
This is not a permissive environment.
What then?
What makes this place special?

Probably it is the teacher.
Undoubtedly it is the teacher.
Families repeatedly tell me they enroll their child in this school because of the teacher.

How does that work?
Yes, I teach a subject.
A rigorous subject.
But mostly, I teach children.

I can think of a number of things I do that enhance the self esteem and intellectual curiosity of children.

1. I call on them only when they want to speak. Never to arouse, embarrass or humiliate.
2. I give half-page tests to everyone so everyone is heard. They each have a voice.
3. We go to lab in pairs almost daily and then report data to the class. We need each other. Without answer books for reference, we need to listen to each other's data-set to find trends and draw conclusions.
4. I set the tone of asking a question but never explaining. There is a respect for student intellect and a confidence that they will figure it out. Prompts are just subtle enough so they think they have done it on their own.
5. I tease them just a bit. Though serious, I play. "Never trust a science teacher." They can't say, "But you said." They have to wonder, "What trick is she playing on us now?" "We fell into her trap? Again!"

It did not happen overnight. Fifty-seven years, actually. That is long enough for the world and my students to teach me something. My first job was teaching geometry in Bellevue High School. Euclidian geometry is argumentation. Deducing consequences from a premise. It is the student's job to figure out the argument. Given. To Prove. You are given the answer at the start of the problem. The quest is to discover how to get there. Teachers listen. They don't read off answers. They listen to arguments.

I think right from the start, the classroom dynamic taught me to listen. After 57 years of daily classroom teaching I may be getting better. I may be better at listening to students.

It has been a long and interesting trip. Studying some metallurgy in grad school. Evening classes. After a full day of high school teaching. Consulting for JPL as the Mars Pathfinder Educator. Weekends. Working in the summer with UNESCO in Zimbabwe, Kenya, and Uganda. Teaching dozens of weekend and week-long summer teacher workshops in South Carolina and Montana. Being a consultant and curriculum designer for Health and Physiology education in Washington, Oregon, Idaho, Montana, and Alaska. Being a summer adjunct University instructor for more than 20 years in Seattle, Idaho and Montana. Teaching teachers. Teaching students every day, every year for 57 years. Observing how learning happens. Becoming aware when real learning isn't happening. When it is just "show." When it is just teacher– pleasing to get a grade. To get a credit. To get a university degree.

Often I get feedback that this type of classroom matters. A student graduating from 8th grade in 2015 sent me this note:

Dear Doc O,
I'm sure you've heard it a lot, but you are an absolutely remarkable teacher. Science class with you was one of the most eye-opening experiences I've had, and your note-taking method for scientific procedures has stayed with me. I feel honored to have had you as a teacher.

Sincerely
G.S.

And from the parents

Dear Doc O,
Thank you for helping to shape our boy. His love of science is due in large part to you and your incredible talents.

Thank you
The Y-S's

Attachment   *Student buy-in*

In this day and age, children often come to school focused on peers and seeking relationships with them. Peer oriented students subtly struggle to control the classroom. I don't let that happen. Right from the start, they can sense that I set the classroom protocol – not them. Roll is taken in a stylized manner. Students follow the prompt.

Often students try to select seats near ranking peers. No, that doesn't happen here. The protocol of the classroom directs their energies – not the peer group.

So there they sit in silence.
I don't say, "Good morning."
I preserve their uncertainty. Their edginess. And their interest.
I look at each one with friendly eyes.
My attention gets their attention.
I need to build on that right away.
This classroom space is new. Arranged differently.
They need direction as they enter, and I am standing there looking fondly at each one. There is no time to build a private peer conversation.
I keep my words to a minimum. I say, "Please be seated."
My few words provide the protocol – the safe boundaries for behavior.
I am not their friend. Not yet their mentor. I am their safe-haven providing security and guidelines about what to do. I have established that the room protocol comes from me, not from peers.

I call roll. Sixteen names in alphabetical order.
I say, "We will do this every day." "Every class."
"How fast can you do it?"
I say the first name and wait.
Silence
"Who is next?"
The person says their name.
I look around. Perhaps I prompt with the next name.
Soon each student is saying their name in turn.
"How fast can you do it?"
I say the first name.
Students call out their name in turn, prompting the slow ones.
Students have figured out what to do without seeming direct
instruction from me.

That starts the tone of the room.
This is not an unstructured environment.
There are rules to follow.
But we have to pay attention to figure them out.

Seats

They are attentive, but they need to be involved.
They want something from me. They want to know where they
will sit. How close to a peer-bond friend will they be? Where will
their "side-conversation" security be? Will I be fair? Arbitrary?
They want nearness to some peers, but not others. They like to
play. Numbers are enchanting to many at this age. Playing with
numbers can powerfully connect them to the classroom protocol
and soften the urgency of peer-attachment.

With a slight smile, I turn on the overhead projector.
I speak as I write and project my words.
"So now there are a bunch of things we have to do."
"Where will we sit?
"How will we take notes?
"Where will we do lab?
"What will we do?

Drawing a plan-view diagram of the seating arrangement on the overhead screen, I say, "What is this?"

They comment.
I don't reply – I just look at them with an appreciative slight smile.
Let the actions speak for themselves.
Data from observation.
Understanding from observation.
That is what we do here.

Without speaking, I take a blank paper and write numbers all over it.
Random numbers.

The students watch.
I unbend a paperclip and set it on the overhead projector so the extended end points to a seat.

"What are the numbers between?"
I point to a student.
The student looks surprised and quizzical.
I point to a different student – and then another.
"What are the numbers between?"
If needed I may say," Give me a range of numbers."
Finally a student understands and responds, "1 to 10."
Holding up my random number paper so the numbers are hidden, I circle a number.

"Who wants this seat?"
Hands go up.
"Write down a number."
"What number have you written?"
I point to students sequentially around the room.
"The number was 6. You are closest."
I write the student's name of the seating chart on the overhead projection.

I pause. Students are getting it.
"Who wants this seat?"
I point to another seat on the chart.
"What are the numbers between?"
I point to a student.

"Write down your number."
"If it isn't written down, you are disqualified."

Magical.
Students figure out what to do.
Without being given a set of instructions.

Experience first, words second.
You are intelligent, valued, enjoyed.
All you have to do is pay attention and you can figure it out for yourself.
We can each figure it out. Together.

The tone of the class is unfolding.
They are learning what is expected of them.
They will ask questions and figure things out and be rewarded with my attention.

It is amazing how rewarding it is to a child, and to a classroom, for the teacher to thoughtfully listen to the comments of a child. A teacher's focused attention makes an emotional bond with the child. It draws the child from peer orientation, at least in the classroom setting. With a teacher's appreciative gaze, I have witnessed the spark of an intellect. I have watched debating skills grow. Comments become more precise, eloquent. It is a joy to watch that happen.

Rules Of Debate

We made good progress yesterday.
We established that being here is satisfying, rewarding.
Being here is fun.
But it is a special type of fun.
It is not a laugh-out-loud joke or a sporting event win.
It is something else.
Motivating.
Deeply satisfying.
Worth coming back to.
Fun.

Children want to grow up. To be seen as being competent.
Worthy. Valued. Enjoyed. They strive because growing into
adulthood is important to them. They acquire a huge vocabulary.
"What's that?" "What's that?" They learn to ride a bicycle. To
jump rope. All without grades. Children don't want friendship
from a teacher. Not buddy-buddy friendship. They don't want
grades. They don't even want praise, really. What they seem to
want is the reflection back on themselves that they are becoming
increasingly competent. Cognitively interesting. More mature.
They can feel themselves growing.

Debate is the reward.
What do students want? Really want?
They want to be listened to. Respected.
Not "show and tell." Not, "my anecdote is like yours." "Better than
yours."

They thrive on a real conversation. Thoughtfully listening. Incorporating and expanding on the ideas of others. Not being judged. Just being interesting – right or wrong. No consequences. Unconditional acceptance after waiting for their turn. Just the development of an idea.

Even quiet children who don't speak much, exhibit attention and sparkly eyes when conversation swirls around them. They laugh at the jokes. The connections. The newfound correlations. But the topic has to be non-trivial. It has to be a serious and sensible topic we are working on. To keep their attention the teacher has to steer the conversation so it remains relevant. Meaningful. Relevant to our work.

Our debate is not helter-skelter. Ideas are not tossed around in a free-for-all. It is more like a court of law. Each contributor is heard thoughtfully. Counter arguments are posed.   Even encouraged. At the same time, each person is recognized as important, appreciated, significant whether right or wrong.

But how to begin?
How to teach them the debate protocol.

My instruction has to be consistent with the end result.
I can't just "tell" them. I want them to reason without being told.
To own the idea. To figure it out. Mostly.
Experience first, words second.

So, I say, "Lets practice."
"A practice topic to see how it goes."

Yes, they are willing to try that.
I write on the overhead screen, "Where are you sitting?"
Keep words to a minimum.
Just pose the topic.

I stand up and look around the room, slightly smiling expectantly.
The teacher poses the question.
It is the student's job to reply.
Thoughtfully.
They know I've got something in mind.
It is their job to struggle toward it.

They want to be here. We have established a beginning
relationship.
By limiting my words, I have their attention.
They are each straining, struggling to figure out what they should
do.
Someone relieves the pressure by saying, "In Seattle."

Quickly I write, "Johnny: Seattle"
I look invitingly around the room and wait.
Others begin to venture.
Timidly.
Copying the lead idea tossed out to them.
As new elaborations are stated, they get written on the overhead.
A repeated idea does not get written.
Glossed over. Almost ignored.
If you want to be rewarded, noticed, think of a new wrinkle – but
stay on the topic.
It doesn't take long for students to catch on.

If someone interrupts another, I loudly say, "OP!" and ignore their comment until my moving finger pointing comes around to them.

I think of it like training a puppy. "Op." Stop action. Don't puddle here. But I still love you. You are so cute".

Students learn to take turns by taking turns.
And by being ignored if they don't.

Most of the time I say nothing. My demeanor communicates interest.
I just point to the next student and paraphrase the idea in my writing on the screen.

Once in a while I stop pointing and interject a new idea or show them they are all focused on the same theory. I slowly steer the comments to notice the desks at which they sit. They begin to notice the shape, height, and raise-lower mechanism. The desks are about 12" deep and 24" wide. They go up and down from 32" to 40". Why?
What were they manufactured for?

"Where are we sitting?"
The focus of comments transforms from geography to mechanics. Students begin to look closely at the desks. They have just one leg and 4 wheels. They have a weighted base and are quite stable. When would they ever have been useful? What were they designed for?

At some point I try to move the discussion around so I can say, "Really?" "That's interesting." "Do you think so?"
Every few days – or few topics, I try to admonish smilingly, "If you don't figure it out, I will punish you." "Yes, I will." "I will **tell** you the answer." "I will simply **tell** you."

"That takes away your chance to think. It is like telling the punch-
line to a joke."
"It takes away the fun."

What a strange idea! Since when is a teacher giving answers a
punishment?
Well it is.
Figuring out is the reward.
Being told is anti-climatic
Being told is punishment.

Another half hour of thinking and conjecture.
Finally someone remembers their uncle in the hospital.
Hospital tables!
We are sitting at hospital tables. The students are agog.
And we figured it out for ourselves!
We didn't have to be told!
Amazing!
And very cool!

We are settling into the pulse, the cadence of the classroom.
The soul of the classroom.
This classroom.

Hot Rods

So, now we have begun.
We chose seats and explored the process of debate.
We learned the format for note taking and have chosen partners
and lab stations – using the number lottery again.

We know how to behave here, but what will we study?
It is time to get into something interesting.
Students are anxious. Pushing for substance.
We are ready to go to work.

Rather than studying "things," or memorizing facts, we collect
data.
Reporting data, we look for trends.
We look for uncontrolled variables.

Class size matters
Since we don't use textbooks, we need to compare data with each
other.
The class can't be too big or it takes too long to record data from
everyone.
The class can't be too small or there is not enough data to feel
confident of trends.

Fourteen students, working in pairs is just about right.
Data from seven labs makes a nice plot on a graph.
It takes patience for students to wait while eight labs report.
Sixteen students are an absolute maximum class size.

So, the flow of a lesson. The teacher sets the task.
"Run Hot Rod races."
"How long will it take a rod to heat?"
"Who can make it heat fastest?"

How can we know?
What are the variables?
The teacher writes the lab on the overhead screen as students copy
and at the same time discuss the variables.

Problem
Equipment
Procedure
Results

We write the heading and together decide what to fill in for this
particular lab activity. The process always follows the same
outline so students know how to work out agreement on what they
will do at lab.

Students go to their chosen labs to explore how to do the task.
The following day class starts with a report from each lab pair on
what they found.
How can you tell if it is getting hot?
What technique did you try? What worked?
Someone notices candles sitting on a shelf.
Can we use wax?
How would that help us tell if a rod was hot?
They go to lab and explore ways to use wax.
Someone finds nails. Can we glue nails on with wax?
When the wax softens enough to drop the nail we know the metal
rod must be hot.
Yes, that works.
Now what? What are the variables?
How many drops of wax?
What should their spacing be?
How should the rod be held?
Do we have to keep the rod end in the burner flame?
Debate. Agreement.
Students negotiate a protocol for telling when rods get hot.

Each day they report data.
We get long lists of numerical data.
There seems to be some agreement, but it is hard to tell.
Perhaps graphing the data will show the trends more sharply.
We decided to use four nails, spaced 3cm apart.
What is the variability of nail-drop time from each lab?
We need to explore the graphical image to decide a confidence interval.

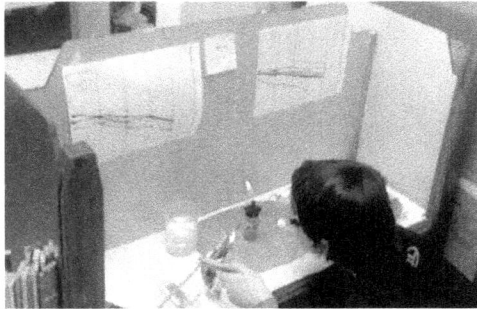

Data reporting. Data tables. Graphing. Argumentation.
That is what we do here.
But the question comes from the teacher.
And the concept emerges from the data.
Experiences first, words and definitions second.

Grades

I have the impression that most classrooms in the nation are driven by "standards" and grading systems. Despite the evidence that these practices interfere with the kind of cognitive development and motivation we most cherish, we continue to do it. I suppose I am passionate about why I still teach. There has got to be something uplifting and of overarching value in what I do. And don't do. I don't give grades.

I give attention.
I give exclamations. "You did it again!" "You connected those ideas!"

Safety

Psychological safety.
I am inviting students to connect ideas.
To be brilliant.
To risk being wrong.
To be thoughtful and interesting.
Not to babble on, but to be precise, crisp, penetrating, eloquent.

How can I ask for brilliance on demand?
How can I require the blinding insight of a newly discovered correlation?

How can I give grades?
The act of grading, of standing in judgment, would destroy the ambience of the class.
Grades would deny the soul of the classroom

Discourse would become contrived. Teacher pleasing. Not authentic.

Teaching, Orchestrating the instructional setting. The ongoing discovery of how to lead students to notice and develop their inner rational self. Not to evaluate or stand in judgment of them.

Report card grades are expected. They are not a surprise.
They are communicated on schedule.
There is nothing special or satisfying about them.
They are subject to being lowered with every reporting period.

A child's self image is more strongly built from the unexpected.
During class debate, when the teacher pauses and says, "That was brilliant!"
"Really insightful!"
The child internalizes the magic of the unexpected moment.
"I am capable." "I am interesting." "I am worth listening to."
The magic moment of spontaneous recognition connects the child to the joy of intellectual discourse.

Grades don't do that.
In fact, they sabotage the very intellectual behavior we are after.
They make it seem that the intellectual struggle was externally motivated.
Very soon it becomes that way.

But that doesn't have to be.
Children are natural explorers. If they feel safe and connected, they are ready to risk. They take delight in discovering relationships and putting data pieces together to make a conceptual whole. It is the teacher's job to make the pieces appropriately sized for the age of the child.
Some children will make the connection. Others will smile when they hear it being made. Either way, the learning unfolds for each student. Associative thinking. Connecting ideas. Not rote memory and regurgitation.

"Good for you."
"What a wonderful idea!"
Every child has the right to wallow in the joy of a wonderful idea without being concerned about class rank or who thought of it first. The point is to think about it at all. To actually think about important ideas. Not to squelch them before they bloom.

I'm not here to make your child an "A" student. I am here to help your child become an interested, interesting human being. Babies are amazing. They develop every day. They seem to become humans on their own. They develop individual personalities. We don't "grade" our baby. We love, value, cherish our clever, interesting baby. Why should we let grades, school grades, interfere with that? Why should we become more focused on measuring achievement than on fostering it? At what point do humans stop being interesting and simply become judged? It doesn't have to be like that. School can partner (informally) with families to keep the magic going. The magic of human development. Bringing home good grades doesn't help. Bringing home interesting ideas does. Actually, we want to tell our child (by our behavior) that we find it satisfying to engage in thoughtful conversations.

Beyond this, grades violate our neuronal pathways.

Grades demand that students represent what they are thinking so we can judge it.
This limits our understanding of cognition to verbal outputs.

In 1926 Graham Wallas discussed four stages of creativity in his essay, THE ART OF THOUGHT. Preparation, incubation, illumination, verification. If we believe this is how creative human thought occurs, as a great many renown psychologists, philosophers and creators do, then we have to allow the possibility that this thought process might happen in our classroom.

Preparation
During preparation, the human accumulates as much as they can from the ideas and intellectual resources around them. It may entail simply paying attention to the swirling discussion in class without actually contributing comments. I believe it is important NOT to call on students until they wish to encode their ideas verbally. Yes, they should pay attention. Yes, they should take notes in their journal. They should gather data at lab. They should input information from as many modalities as possible.

Incubation
I don't assign homework. I don't gather students at the end of each class period to bring "closure" on their lab activity. I let the odd bits of information dangle and stew around. Einstein and others describe combining ideas almost unconsciously without the mediation of words. I let the mind disengage from the task in the evening. I let them turn to other tasks such as math homework. Idea connection often comes as the student drifts toward sleep. Unfinished ideas are not lost. They are just not connected yet. They must not be forced or demanded by grades on a report card.

Illumination
The flash of insight comes to only a few students. Their zestful comments the next day in class model intellectual behavior for other students. Everyone benefits. But illumination can't be forced. It can only be appreciated. We celebrate thoughts from our students and we honor creative connections made by famous scientists in the past.

Verification
Once a wonderful connection has been posed, it may be possible to design a lab activity to investigate it further. We all join in to gather the data to see how the idea unfolds.

Wallas reminds us that these four types of thinking continually overlap as we work on larger conceptual understanding. We must allow this to happen. Schools should not get in the way of human intellectual development. Grades interfere.

I don't give grades.

Images

What is on the wall?
Data graphics.

We have solved the issue of buy-in. Students want to be here and they welcome engaging in thoughtful debate. But is that enough?

We need to consider how students actually learn. How can they know if they have learned? If they have crafted an understanding for themselves? It is strange. We often tell ourselves that we understand.

We nod our head when we hear someone describe something. Yet, when we are asked to explain in writing, we are often at a loss.

I frequently give half page tests. I cut an 8x11 paper in half and silently distribute a paper to each child. Oh oh! They don't know what is coming. Often I ask an odd question. The purpose is to probe for prior knowledge without telling them the forthcoming topic.

For example:
Johnny has a pet rock. He likes to care for his pet rock. It is winter. He brings a quilt out and covers his pet. How long will it take for his pet rock to warm up?

I am probing for understanding of metabolism. Perhaps something about ambient temperature. I read the answers as I collect the papers but I do not give feedback. I do not tell them if they are right or wrong. Once in a while someone crafts an unusual answer which I may comment on. Mostly they know whether they felt adequate or not. Later in a lesson flow, the idea may come up again which allows me to then say, "Remember the pet rock question?" "What would you say now?

Often the half-page test introduces a topic. On rare occasion it asks for knowledge. For example: "Write the equation for photosynthesis."

Again I give no feedback. They whisper to their neighbor. They know if they got it right. If not, they practice the answer so they won't be caught by it next time.

They know if they are learning. I don't have to stand in judgment.

But there is more to learning than feedback. There is more than being willing. Thought needs to be given to how human minds acquire knowledge and how they synthesize that knowledge into big concepts. How do our minds explore properties of "stuff"?

The verbal part of our intellect can report to us what we can put into words. But we know more than that. Brilliant minds such as Albert Einstein and Arthur Koestler talk about knowledge that came to them without words. Images played a large part in their thinking. Where do images enter the classroom activity? How do we use images? What kinds of images might we create?

It is just so easy to begin with words. To ask a question. The response comes in words and often in numbers. OK, but then what?

"How hot can you heat water?"
I just ask the question. They have no idea that I am drawing them into the concept of Latent Heat, of heating-cooling curves and their relation to atmospheric pressure, or the how the Earth is driven by its geodynamo.

They just take it at face value.
"How hot can you heat water?"
"What are the variables?"
"Does amount matter?"
"Does heat source matter?"
"What variables must we agree to control as we set up our lab apparatus?"

So we all write up the lab as I model the task on the overhead projector.
Problem: How hot can we heat water?
Equipment: …… We make a list as students call out suggestions
Procedure: … Again, a list of steps thrashed out in class dialogue
Results: After seeming to negotiate I steer the conclusion to taking temperature every 15 seconds. Students can do it and this timing keeps them focused. No time for peer interaction. We have to work efficiently!
The next day, after taking roll, we write:, "Class Data" in our journals and prepare a grid-work to accept data from each lab. Each and every student does this and I do it too. "What ever I write on the board, you write." Eight labs report their data as I call on them in numerical order. Each student has a full record of all the findings.

Conclusions?
Time for discussions.
We find patterns in the data.
We find agreement.
We find outliers. What are possible uncontrolled variables?
Based on the discussion, we agree we need to try again.
We need more refined data. More controlled variables.
What if we started with really cold water? Ice water?

A second day. A third day.
More reporting time and class discussion.
Students are making progress but it is not good enough.

I can tell from their conversation that they think they have an answer. A numerical answer.
They do not realize that there is an underlying concept.

We have been using words and numbers. They have taken us as far as they can.
We need an image.

Time to graph the data.
Much of the time we plot everyone's data and look for confidence intervals.
Not this time.
We need to plot a single data set.
You should probably plot your own set, but if you like another lab's better it is OK to plot theirs.
That's odd.
Aren't students supposed to do their own work?
Well, yes.
But what is the point of "pitting" one lab against another?
We are trying to uncover truth from the world.
It really doesn't matter where the data came from so long as it is a single full set.

It is strange how we teach science.
"**You** had better get the right answer."
Rather than, "Can we figure out what the world is telling us?"

I believe comments of, "Oh, I see, my ring was higher than yours – an uncontrolled variable." Are much more valuable that saying, "My data is better than yours."

Everyone plots a data set. Time vs. temperature. All the graphs are laminated and posted at each lab. Everyone can see them. Compare them. Value them.
That's what should be on the wall – our interesting work that might spark a conversation or build a memory.

So, what is the shape? Do we see something more in the data from making an image of it? Well, yes. Most graphs have two plateaus. A high plateau and a low plateau.
It sort of looks like the letter Z. A hieroglyph Z. We call it a Z-for Zorro. Who was Zorro? Some students don't know but the others quickly fill them in about the comic character.
A memory hook. A playful memory hook.
Why must science be serious and sober all the time?

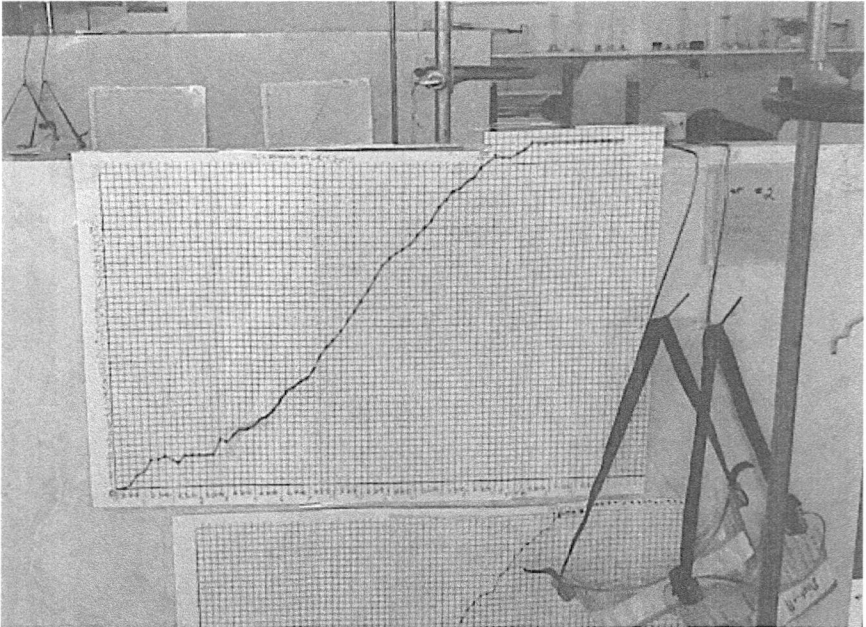

So, a Z has a high plateau and a low plateau.
Are they all the same?
Is there a range of variability?
What could be causing that?

Rousing discussion, but here I have to prompt a little.
What was the weather like? Did that matter?
What if I did this experiment in the mountains?
Why do Brownie mixes have different cooking directions for high altitude cooking?

"When I was your age, I went camping in the mountains. I had to cook a pot of pasta for the group. But it never cooked. I finally buried it in the ground – embarrassed at my ineptness."

People are climbing Mt. Everest today. Can they sterilize their water by boiling it?

Captain Cook found the elevation of coastal mountains by taking the temperature of boiling water at the top.

How does that work?

Finally they are ready to be told. They have enough discrepant information to seek an answer. They are interested. Ready for a concept. But presented with age-appropriate terms and detail.

Atmospheric pressure controls boiling temperature.
The water molecules have to push up against the atmosphere to boil – to jump out of the beaker. More atmospheric weight takes more energy – thus a higher temperature.

We talk about that for a while and consider many scenarios.

Time for a half-page test.
"Where on Earth would you be if your high plateau were way up here?"
(Death Valley? The Dead Sea?)

"Where would you be if the high plateau were way down here?
(on top of a mountain)
"What about a triple-point? When would water boil as soon as it
melts?
(Space or Mars?)

They see if they can figure it out. But they aren't graded.
They converse.
"I said …."
"Really, I don't think so."

Knowledge should promote conversations,
Knowledge shouldn't judge people.

So, lets think about imagery.
Imagery.
Images of places. What is it like there?
Images in time. When did that happen?
Images correlate. What events happened together?
Why? Cause and effect?
What to look for next time.

Multiple Images

Image comparison.

I don't explain.
I don't point out that we haven't controlled variables very well.
I don't discuss that we don't have a comparison.
Proper science requires more than a single experiment.
And it requires that comparisons are presented on matching displays.
I can watch for that as we go along. But kids don't need it yet.

Kids don't quibble with the procedural details.
They just enjoy the "rush" of lighting alcohol burners.
They enjoy getting data that makes them feel quite grown up.
They respond to my next question, trusting that I will lead them properly.

And so I say, "Z for Zorro."
The image shaped our understanding of the verbal – numerical data.
The image suggested intriguing questions.
We understand more after creating the image.

Do other substances do that?
Do they make Z for Zorro's?
Do they make plateaus? Two of them?

Lets try salt water.
What do you predict will happen"
Actually, you have three choices: the same, higher, or lower.
For each of the plateaus.

I ask the question on a half-page test so they have to commit to a guess.
Right or wrong. It doesn't matter.

Together we write up the lab, "How hot can you heat SALT water?"
What are the variables?
We had better see how much we can dissolve in water first.
A preliminary lab.

Having determined 20gms in 100 ml of water, we begin.
Gather data.
Report
Graph on a matching coordinate system.
Debate. Argue.
Doing the lab several times over, we find the high plateau is consistently higher than boiling plain water. The low plateau is consistently lower.
We get a double Z for Zorro.
So? Do I notice any students grasping the importance?

Half-page tests.
Questions to think about.
Why do we put salt on roads and sidewalks in winter?
Why do farmers in Wenatchee spray apple blossoms with water on freezing nights?
Why do farmers, in Wisconsin, in winter, store piles of apples in underground root cellars, nested around barrels of rain water?

Homework. Freeze an apple at home and bring it in to the science room.
Ewww! After freezing, apples become putrid!
Apples have sugar. Where would sugar water plateaus be?
I simply tell them. Sugar plateaus are between salt and plain water: both high and low. How does that help? The exchange of heat is mysterious.

To comprehend Latent Heat we have to experience it happening.
Test tubes of Sodium Thiosulphate take heat in from a burner while crystals melt.
Drop in a single crystal, and the test tube gives the heat back to my hand as crystals form.
Exothermic.
The heat was stored in the liquid.
It had to get rid of the heat to change back to solid.
Hidden heat that I can't measure.
Latent Heat.
Magic!

We talk over the half-page questions.
But, these are children.
They need a memory reference.
How do you make old-fashioned ice cream?
Salt and ice-water in a large baggie. Sugar and cream mix in an inside baggie.

 Salt water "wants" to be liquid at a lower temperature. It doesn't "want" to be ice. In order for ice to melt it has to grab heat from somewhere (to make the phase change from solid to liquid). It grabs heat from the cream. As the cream cools, it solidifies into ice-cream!

OK. Lets try that.   Yummy

<u>But, Does It Work?</u>

We have a classroom protocol.
For writing notes, recording data and graphing.
For dialogue.
Reasoning.
Not necessarily agreement, but for being heard.

Does the method work?
Does the method produce learning?
Superior learning?
Better than rote memorization?

Well, first of all, every student is engaged.
Focused.
They don't drowse in class.
They enter the room and rapidly get their notes open and ready.
Students are not simply reading and intellectually drifting.
Everyone is alert.
Ready for a challenge.
Debate.
What question will the teacher throw at us this time?
Students expect to draw on past information.
To make unusual connections.
To live with non-closure, uncertainty.
Ready to pounce on an idea.
So learning is anticipated.
Every day.

There are many ways to evaluate learning.
We can observe student behavior.
Their attitude.
Do the students feel brilliant?
Insightful?
Do they love being here?

We can explore student knowledge.

We can examine teacher intention.
What does the teacher have in mind for students to comprehend?

In this classroom, each year is structured around an overarching concept.
Heat and Temperature, for instance.
The year begins by exploring activities underpinning the concept Latent Heat.
Lessons move to Specific Heat, calories and Calories, Counter-current Heat Exchange, the vascular bed and heart structure, and finally, the earth as a heat engine.
There are a few intervening units of work such as an inquiry on the Periodic Table to provide background for understanding equations for photosynthesis and metabolism. A magical 3-week puzzle mixing colored liquids leads to discovery of acids and bases.
About 5 weeks in the Fall are spent on an engineering event selected from topics in the news. A few recent events include:
Archimedes and Archimedes palimpsest
Great Wheels
Wind farms
Baby carriages
Drones
Wildfire
Every year is different, but projects always include Potential – Kinetic Energy, bearings, bushings, friction, and tool use such as saws, hammers, glue guns, drill press, rubber bands, motors springs and junk. Lots of junk.

Students like novelty. They like to think they are studying different topics. But, how do we create the opportunity for associative thinking? The units of work have to be juxtaposed so students can make connections.

To understand a future unit on changes of the amount of Oxygen in the atmosphere, it is helpful to be familiar with the equation for photosynthesis. When hydrocarbons (or carbohydrates) are combined with Oxygen, Carbon Dioxide is formed. So, later in the year when we are told the Oxygen in the atmosphere decreased, I can probe and prompt asking where was the fuel? Where was the Methane? What earthly process sent large pulses of hydrocarbons into the atmosphere to draw down the Oxygen and raise the Carbon Dioxide?

Facts, in and of themselves, are not wonderful.
Memorizing textbook answers is not the same as relating ideas.
The ideas have to be internalized.
Discussed.
Reflected upon.
Argued about.
Disagreed with.
Left dangling and called upon at odd unexpected moments.
The teacher has to set the stage with bits of knowledge that can be associated.
Associative thinking is where the "Aha's" come from.

So, what bits of information do I solidly place in the mind of the student throughout the year focused on Heat and Temperature?

We must remember the concept Latent Heat. Our data graphic (hieroglyph) Z-for-Zorro helps with that.

We need to revisit the equations for photosynthesis and
metabolism/burning fairly frequently.
Everyone should thoroughly understand the structure of the heart
and its importance to the cardiovascular system as a lens through
which to view future lessons of the flow of evolution through time.

But, how thorough is thorough?
What are the expectations for this age child?
Actually, this method of discussion produces remarkable learning.
Far above our expectations.
Without homework
Simply from being enticed and enfolded in rousing discussion.

≈

A Parent sent this note:

Hello Dr. Olson

I just wanted to share the attached diagram L… drew this weekend. As it happens, on Sunday she was sitting in church and quietly drawing to pass the time. Normally she draws flowers, animals, people, landscapes, and so on, but this time, I noticed she was drawing something pretty different: a diagram of the human heart. After the service ended, she was going to recycle it, but I asked if I could keep it. I asked her about it, and she happily expounded on whatever I asked about: the ductus arteriosus, the "upsie" and "downsie", etc. She talked about the "four gurglies" and a number other things she recalled from class. Throughout her whole impromptu presentation of this diagram, she was quite animated.

This was a wonderful experience for me as a parent. It's great to hear my children talk about the things that interest them, and doubly so when I don't know (or recall) much about the topic myself. And here it was particularly neat to catch a glimpse of L…'s interest in science — perhaps a deeper interest than I'd previously realized. L…'s really enjoying her class with you this year, and I hear quite a bit about science from her after school, but seeing this sketch made me see that she's continuing to mull over science class material long after the class. If she continues to pursues her interest in science as she grows up, I suspect I'll be able to entertain her someday with a story about this diagram.

Anyway, I thought you might enjoy seeing this. I also wanted to say thanks for stimulating this interest in L…. Both A… and L… have heard me say many, many times how lucky they are to be getting such a great exposure to scientific thinking, practice, and topics at such an early age.

Best,
Jan M.

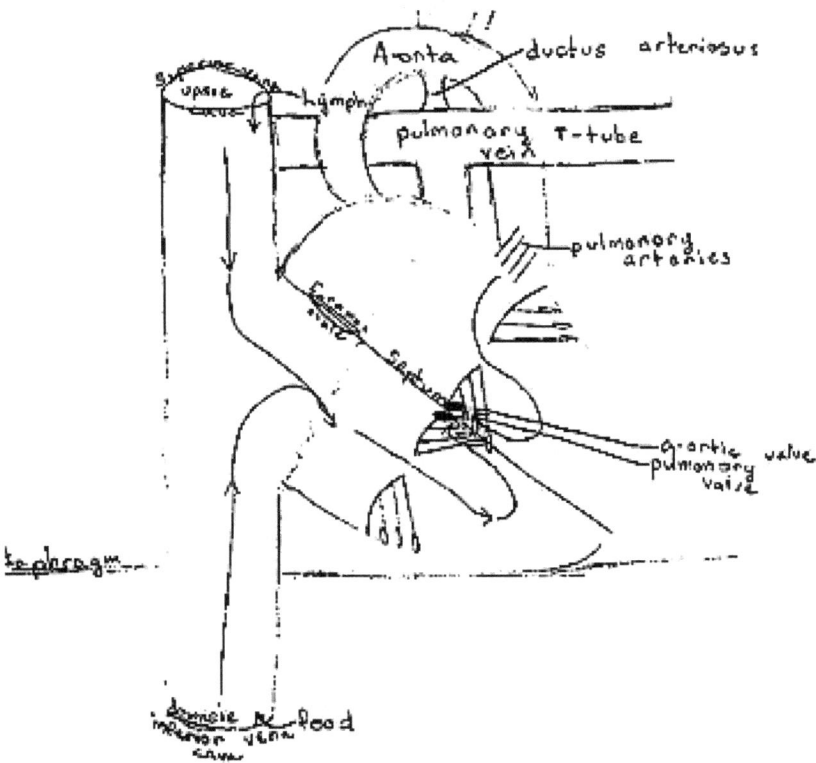

And the school Principal commented:
Many thanks for sharing this with me. These are the stories and
informal feedback pieces that confirm that what we do has
meaning, purpose, and impact for the children we serve.
Congratulations, and thank you for continuing to be such a
difference in the lives of so many students!

Sincerely,
Michael M.

Head of School

Some students learn and remember more than a hundred terms of
structure and function related to the heart. Even the slowest
student in the class has enormous familiarity with the topic from
simply taking notes and being surrounded by the swirling class
discussion
Our four chamber heart.
We know the structure.
But is it always that way?
The magic of birth.
What change must take place in a minute or so while the baby
moves from living in a fluid environment to an air-breathing
environment?
What if those changes don't happen?
What is a "birth defect"?
What sorts of irregularities are sometimes found?
We have learned a great deal about a four chamber heart.
Missing septums sometimes leave the baby with a three chamber
heart.
Is that ever good?
Useful?
What kind of critters have three chamber hearts?
Two chambers?
 We dissected gills in the Counter-current unit to explore how
oxygen enters blood. Two chamber hearts work sometimes.

Leave the questions open.
Unfinished.
Ready for future connections.
"Aha's"

So the lessons are not just a string of topics.
Not just a list of clever lab activities.
Ideas are planted in the mind of students in a careful sequence to enhance understanding of the year-long conceptual scheme. They are resurrected and cultivated at periodic intervals to refresh and enlarge their meaning. Without really noticing, students acquire a web of concepts to provide ammunition for moments of brilliance.
Associative thinking.
Connecting ideas.
Emerging understanding.

Things Are Not As They Seem

I want to teach some earth science.
That is a bit difficult.
Students are used to gathering data and making sense out of it.
But what if the data doesn't make sense?
What if things are not as they seem?
What if I need more time, centuries, to gather trends in the data?
What if it appears that one thing is going on, yet it is quite another?
Does the fly on an elephant think he is in a forest? Does he know those are hairs?

The Earth looks flat, but it isn't.
The sun moves across the sky. But it doesn't
The data was so consistent, so compelling that society championed huge projects to celebrate it. They built pyramids. What were they thinking?

The sun moves back and forth creating seasons. Doesn't it?
What did "transits" of Venus tell us about perfect heavenly motion?
Galileo and Copernicus were persecuted by those who knew the data.
But data is tricky.
Data remains, but how we interpret it changes.
We see something happen today.
But what does it mean?
Really mean?
In the larger scheme of how the Earth-machine works.

Gold weighs more in Alaska but it is up in the mountains.
Is there more pull of gravity high up in mountains?

Magnetic North moves. Fast.
How is that possible?

Sea level changes. Oh no! isn't that bad?
Earthquakes happen. Oh no!
Volcanoes erupt disrupting air traffic.
Global warming!
"Ice age" river freezing is coming by 2030 so the news from
Northumbria says.
We will soon be revisiting "Hans Brinker and the Silver Skates."
The Themes will freeze over. So will the Hudson.

It is alarming!
It seems chaotic.
We are at the mercy of each new "politically correct" explanation.

Information overload!
How can I approach the topic?
How can I orchestrate the same intrinsic motivation and
intellectual exploration that sparked the physics units? How can I
avoid simply dispensing information? Where in the morass of
earth science data are the "hooks" where students become involved
and thoughtful? Where can they question, discover, argue, while
avoiding "politically correct" explanations influenced by modern
politics?

Earth science is an odd subject to teach.
It seems straight forward. But it isn't.
We walk on it. We look at surroundings.
But we don't see.
We don't see changes through time. We don't live long enough.

Isn't it amazing that Stonehenge has holes filled with chalk
showing a seventeen year lunar cycle when the average life span
was to age seventeen. How can we gather data beyond our years?

We now know the UK was a couple of New Zealand – like islands
near the South Pole not so long ago. (We call them Avalonia and
Ganderia). Scotland was part of eastern Canada at that time.
Really?
How do we know that?

Well, we have to know what south sea ribbon -continents are like.
What kind of landforms do they contain ? Typically they have
Rhyolite volcanic mountain peaks and lahar mudflows. Lots of
seashore and clam shells and cold-water sea urchins. I have to
understand the attributes of ribbon-continents to recognize a
graveyard of their churned up parts.

I wonder if my students would be patient enough to listen to a
description.
Although I only occasionally tell stories, I think I will try it.

A South Sea messed up ribbon continent.

New Zealand. What would it be like? A world away.

Stretching more than a thousand miles across the Southern Ocean, but only about 200 miles wide, New Zealand has thousands miles of coastline. A rugged landscape. Mountain ranges, coastal plains, volcanic plateaus and fjords. And it is active. There are underground rivers carving limestone caverns. Within the last two million years, mountains uplifted to almost ten thousand feet. The Taupo Caldera produced earth's largest eruption in the past 70,000 years. And things slide - on fault lines. The Alpine Fault, 300 miles long, is said to be the longest straight line on the planet. It lurches sideways averaging about ten feet per year.

As the land moves, living things are entombed in the soil. Cobb valley near Nelson has sedimentary rocks formed 540 to 360 million years ago that contain fossils of trilobites that lived then. Whales, dolphins and penguins lived 25 million years ago only to be preserved in submerged limestone now found around North Otago. The land must have moved from polar latitudes toward the equator because some trilobites lived in cold polar regions but later fossils are of tropical critters such as reptiles, wading birds, crocodiles and even palm trees and coconuts.

And living things are still being trapped in the soil. Mountains erupt on a regular basis. In 1886 Mt Tarawera erupted, sending clouds of ash and rock five miles into the sky. Steam, mud and ash devoured towns as they were completely buried by the falling mud. We wonder if some day we will find any of the hundred missing bodies: human fossils.

But other events also stop living things in their tracks and entomb them eventually turning them into fossils. On Christmas Eve, 1953 a great disaster occurred Of the 151 people who died, twenty were never found. Fossils, left for future scientists to discover. What happened? An express train was taking passengers from Wellington to Auckland when it was caught in a huge mud slide (Lahar) from Mt Ruapehu. The mud crashed into the train just as it crossed the Whangaehu River bridge. Cars were tossed into the churning mud and enveloped forever.

So, New Zealand is lovely, but rather churned up. Mountains rise and weather down. Rivers carry huge amounts of sediment to the sea. Dead bodies are caught in the collecting soil and preserved as fossils. The sediment often gets squished as land slides and crumples up and the fossils go with it.

What an amazing churned up puzzle. How will future geologists ever untangle the sequence of events? How will they know which came first? Mud looks about the same from eon to eon. Maybe the type of fossils will give a clue.

So now, are those landforms found in the UK?
Well yes. People began to notice strange soil layers and fossilized sea shells.
That is why the academic discipline of Geology began in the UK.
It is an amazing story of a brilliant mind being in the right place at the right time.
And the story leads to a historic graphical image.
A powerful image that we might use to organize our thinking about how the earth works.
We need that image to develop our lessons. To create debate. To experience exhilarating "aha's". It is worth our time to listen to another story. It has human interest. Pathos. So maybe I can sustain their interest for a couple of days.

I need to try because the image is central to our progress.
I need to have students buy-in to John Phillips' diagram of the history of land life.
It provides our frame of reference. It encapsulates our understanding.
Our questions. Our memory

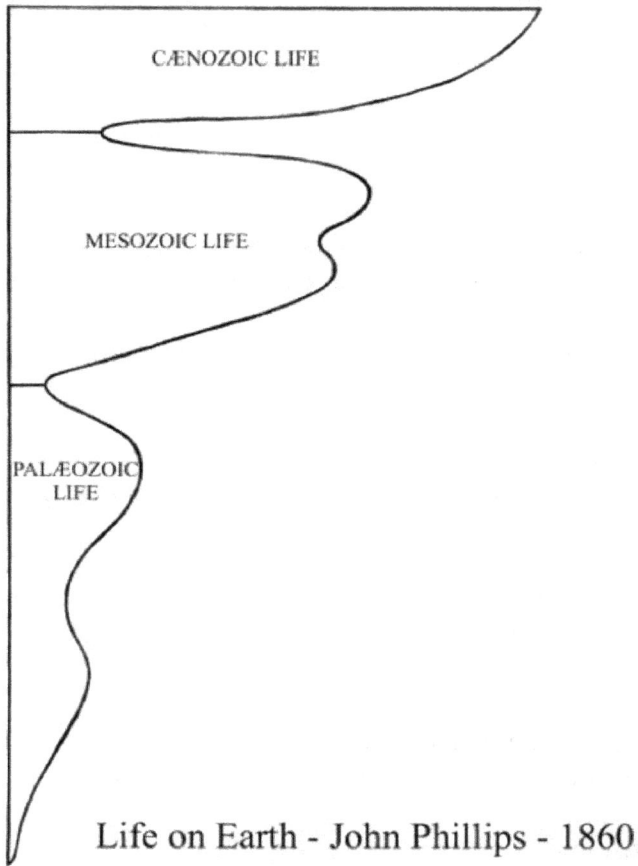

CÆNOZOIC LIFE

MESOZOIC LIFE

PALÆOZOIC
LIFE

Life on Earth - John Phillips - 1860

I have to tell the story.
But stories get dull very quickly.
I have to have a quick cadence and a rapid punch line.
Leave out the details.
Just enough to carry their interest along.
What I am after is the punch-line.
Phillips' graph.
That will become our tool for the rest of the year.

William Smith

The context: time, place, setting

From Wikimedia Commons, the free media repository
Author   Cnbrb

By the 1700's the little ice age left the UK land soggy. Enclosure Acts (1701-1800) would help organize the soggy fields. People wouldn't spend money on commonly held community property like village greens. But privately held land was worth an investment. Land had to be surveyed. Fields had to be drained so crops that were planted would thrive.

England cut down forests. There was competition between ship building and metal forging for the use of wood. In 1558, Queen Elizabeth stopped the cutting of timber to simply use as fuel for the making of iron. A new fuel was needed. In1711, Abraham Darby used coal for the smelting of iron. By 1760, coal was a popular fuel for forging iron. The Industrial Revolution was begun. People wanted coal to build large fires so they could smelt iron. But how could heavy coal be moved to the foundries? A great many canals were built from 1770 onward to move the heavy coal.

Unless they had things to move, people walked. Lewis and Clark walked across North America. No one thought it unusual.

Alexander von Humboldt walked across South America. That's what people did. Walking was good. It kept your head close to the soil. People looked at rocks as they stumbled over them. You couldn't collect rocks riding in a wagon or stage coach.

Young years

Into this setting a baby was born. The year was 1769. The baby was destined to become self-educated, well known, wealthy, robbed, imprisoned, and finally awarded the highest medal.

In 1769 a baby was born in Churchill, UK. His name was William Smith. The son of the local blacksmith. By the age of 7 or 8, William's father had died and he went to live with his uncle on a dairy farm. He milked cows and sold butter. Butter was weighed using local fossils called "pound stones." They were remarkably uniform, nearly all weighing about 22oz. He knew they looked like sea urchin shells but people thought God was playing tricks by leaving shell shaped rocks around the inland countryside. He began to collect them and carefully label where they were found.

Pound Stones

After he learned to read he walked many miles to purchase books. Mathematics mostly. Geometry and then Surveying.

When William was 18, he had just read his third book – on surveying. The village invited a surveyor to town to help them determine field boundaries for their land enclosure project. William was very interested in the project and the well-known surveyor needed help. After helping for just one day, William was hired. That was amazing! Being the son of a local farming family, he never anticipated having a paying job any time in his life. William was really good with geometry. He learned quickly and soon became a proficient surveyor. Enclosures were happening up and down the central UK countryside and he was much in demand.

Most enclosures 1700 – 1850 = shaded area
William lived in Churchill

www4.uwsp.edu/english/rsirabia/notes/212/enclosureActs.pdf

He walked from town to town with the master surveyor, laying out field boundaries and measuring for fences. Walking allowed him to look closely at rocks.

He was good at visualizing in 3-D and often helped design ways to drain water from the land. He became well known and started to earn a lot of money. All the while, he collected fossils and recorded their locations and his discoveries in his daily journal.

In 1791, he was sent south to Somerset to make a valuation survey of the Sutton Court estate. An earlier owner, geologist John Strachey had made preliminary sketches of the property.

Building on Strachey's work he added to his knowledge of the property by working in one of the older mines: the Mearns Pit. He studied the strata, collected fossils, made maps and took copious notes of what he saw. He agreed with previous geologists that there seemed to be a uniform easterly dip to all the beds of rock. He was able to make a detailed assessment of the potential value of coal in several regions of the property.
Strachey sketch

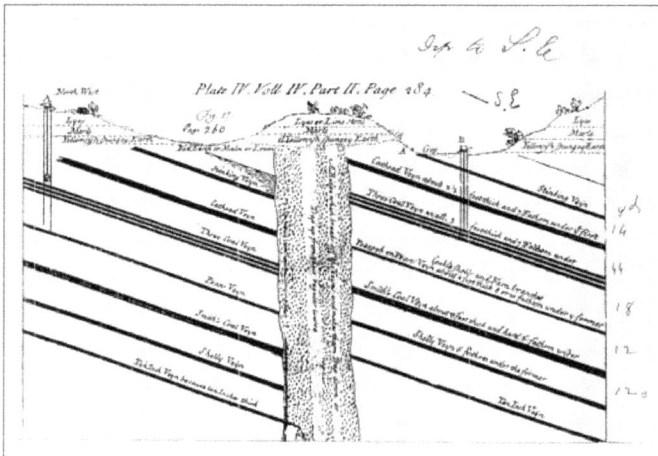

John Strachey's sketch showed coal layers on nearby properties and why he thought there was coal to be found on his estate.

https://www.geolsoc.org.uk/Geoscientist/Archive/July-2007/Smiths-other-debt

People wanted to make money selling the coal to Bath, Wiltshire, and London. The roads were in very bad condition and coal wagons couldn't travel over them. They needed a canal to deliver the heavy coal to market. In 1793, William Smith was hired to survey a canal to deliver the coal and his report includes observations which helped him formulate his strata theory. His notes show he noticed rock strata matched from place to place and could be identified by the fossils they contained. His beautiful Somerset Canal is still in use today.

Laying out a canal meant looking closely at rock layers. You could predict what you would find by matching layers from place to place. Canals were not very deep – usually about 3 to 5 feet. A man could stand up in most canals. You didn't need much water to float a heavy barge loaded with coal.

William Smith became wealthy enough to be able to purchase a nice estate near the town of Bath. He was invited to join the civic society of land-owning leaders of Bath even though he was from a humble farming family.

After leaving the canal job, he traveled all over England surveying and determining where canals should be dug. He was often invited to visit manor houses in various parts of the UK to oversee surveying tasks.

William Smith had an idea.

William knew the land and the layers. He had kept a careful daily journal of where he walked and what he saw. He collected a vast array of fossils (more than 2,500) and had carefully labeled where each was found. He had surveyed coalmines and had recorded the layers where fossils were found as mine pits were dug. He knew the "under-side" of England.

Many people were trying to figure out the rationale for the crumpled hillsides. They began giving names to layers of rocks. But rocks changed. Sometimes they seemed to be sandy beaches and then changed to mud flows and volcanic rock. Which came first? How could they know? The layers were often given names of the local native tribes where the rocks were found. Silures and Silurian. Ordovices and Ordovician. People argued over names. People argued over the order of sequence. Sometimes they were jumbled. Sometimes they were upside-down."

GEOLOGIC TIME CHART
  Quaternary
   Tertiary
  Cretaceous
   Jurassic
   Triassic
   Permian
 Pennsylvanian
 Mississippian
  Devonian
   Silurian
  Ordovician
  Cambrian

William Smith recognized that the rock types changed in unpredictable ways. In 1796 Smith realized that fossils didn't change. Although rock types were sand and then mud and then rock, the fossils left from life forms that lived there remained the same. Fossils always were found in the same order. One above the next in the rock layers. The order was always the same, no matter what type of rock it was. You could tell which came first by noticing the type of fossil found there. You could tell it all over England where ever you went. It was an exciting idea! At the Swan Inn in Dunkerton on December 2nd, 1796, Smith wrote the idea down in his journal. But he didn't tell anyone.
Finally, in 1799, he went to dinner with two wealthy friends (Richardson and Townsend) and told them his idea. "Oh right!" They were supposed to believe that! Well, if William Smith was right, he should be able to prove it. The next day the three men took a stagecoach to a nearby hill. They stopped the coach from time to time and said, "OK, what fossil will we find here?" William got out and after digging around, found a fossil. Every single time he was right! Oh my goodness! William Smith could tell the order of the layers from the fossils!

They went to Townsend's manor house for dinner. Richardson took pen and paper and wrote while William Smith paced the floor dictating his knowledge. After many hours, they had three copies of William Smith's profound idea.

They were so excited that they told many others who were working on the same puzzle. They spoke at meetings and shared their enthusiasm. It was an exciting time. People were figuring things out.

University of New Hampshire copy of the document written by Richardson 1799

http://www.unh.edu/esci/WilliamSmiths-StrataIdentified/iii/table.html

Then William Smith had another idea. He could make a map. If someone would provide a really good map of the UK, William could color the locations of where he found each fossil in his collection. Everyone would be able to see where the layers outcropped and where coal might be found. There was money to be made, so many people would want to buy the map. When he told people his plan, they cheered him on. There was great interest in purchasing such a map, even though it would be expensive.

William was a perfectionist. He wanted the map to be precise and beautiful. He found a printer who would provide maps and wait for payment until they were sold. William wanted them colored in 20 tints in a precise way with colors fading upward in each layer. He wanted the map be big. Nine feet tall by six feet wide. That would take a lot of paper (15 engraved sheets per map) and a lot of time. Between surveying jobs, William worked on his maps. He finally had a bunch (perhaps 400 of them) ready for sale in 1815.

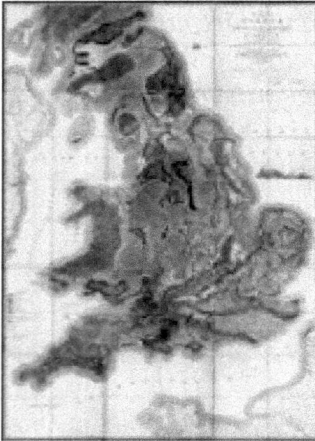

Copy of one of William Smith's original maps
#a65 original 1916

But – people were impatient. They knew a map was coming. They wanted it now! One of the wealthy, famous people interested in William's idea went to the print shop and looked at William's map. He had the printer make some maps for him. He colored his maps (probably using a lot of William's data) and sold them first. By the time William's maps were available, no one would buy them. They already had purchased what they needed. William went broke.

In 1818 he sold his precious fossils to London's Natural History Museum. His exacting collections of 2,657 specimens, 693 species were sold at a price of £700, to the British Museum. Each specimen carries Smith's label showing where it was found and has a special number assigned to it by Smith. You can see the collection today in the Paleontology Department of the Natural History Museum in London. His collection was magnificent. Even so, he was eventually put in prison. Debtor's prison, for 80 days, while everything else he had was sold to pay his debts. When he got out of prison he was impoverished. He got in a stagecoach and rode north, disappearing into the countryside. A broken man.

For the next seven years he wandered around doing odd jobs of surveying and land draining. He occasionally gave public lectures. In 1820 Scarborough asked him to improve the town's water supply. In 1821 he published a Geological Map of Yorkshire. He set up the famous rotunda geologic museum in Scarborough. In 1828 Sir John Johnstone of Hackness Hall, near Scarborough, gave him a job as land steward. Famous geologists regularly visited him but he felt excluded from his rightful place in geologic society.

http://en.wikipedia.org/wiki/Rotunda_Museum

In 1831, when the first Wollaston medal was to be awarded, people finally decided they had been unfair.

William Smith was found taking care of the large estate in the northern part of the country. He was brought to London and awarded the first Wollaston prize. In 1832, King William IV gave him a pension of £100 per year for the rest of his life. He was also given an Honorary Doctorate of Letter (LL.D from Trinity College, Dublin for his brilliant work – even though he had never been allowed to go to college.

John Phillips

The nephew with another idea

Meanwhile, back in Churchill, William Smith's sister fell in love and got married to a Revenue & Customs officer with a good education. The family moved as her husband changed jobs, living in Marden, (where John was born in 1800), Midford (near Bath), and Deddington, Oxfordshire. After both his parents died in 1808, John and his sister went to live with their uncle, William Smith. William Smith paid John's tuition at a very good school for five years and then sent him to study with his friend and scholar, Richardson. John Phillips never went to college but said he felt his time with Richardson was a college level education.

 Phillips's formal education ceased after the age of 15. For seventeen years, Phillips accompanied Smith on his surveying projects. He moved to the northern part of the country when Smith was released from prison Being a young man with time on his hands, when his uncle spoke with local land owners about surveying, John asked if he could arrange their fossil collection for them. He became really, really knowledgeable about fossils. In the spring of 1824 Smith went to the museum at York to deliver some lectures on geology and, of course, John Phillips went along. John asked if he could arrange their fossils. He so impressed them that he was offered the job of "keeper of the

Yorkshire museum" even though he had not even been to college. He soon became the secretary of the Yorkshire Philosophical Society. By 1831 he was working for University College London. In 1834 he became professor of geology at King's College London and was elected a fellow of the Royal Society, and at the same time continued his post at York. In 1856, he became a professor and keeper of Clarendon Laboratory and the University Observatory at Oxford, a post he kept until his death. Although he never went to college, he received honorary degrees of LL.D. from Dublin and Cambridge, and D.C.L. from Oxford. In 1845 he was awarded the Wollaston Medal by the Geological Society of London.

All the while he continued to study fossils and published memoirs and papers. He was uneasy with the rock-system names that were based on specific regions of the country. He liked Smith's principle of identifying rock formations with fossils. He noticed the fossils changed as you climbed the hill.

File:Blue lias cliffs at Lyme Regis.jpg From Wikimedia Commons, the free media repository

English: Sea cliff made up of an alternation of Lower Jurassic dark claystones and limestones of the Blue Lias Formation at Lyme Regis, Dorset, UK.
Author: Michael Maggs

The fossils get more numerous and larger as you moved up layer upon layer. Then, suddenly, no fossils. Why weren't there any fossils in that layer?
Had everything gone extinct?
Why were the fossils so different in the next layers up?
Why did they become more numerous and larger again?
But how can we describe how the fossils differ?

Phillips thought a naming system for rock layers ought to reflect changes in the history of life. In 1841 John Phillips published his landmark diagram showing three major geological eras: "Old life: the Palæozoic (or "The Age of Fishes"), "Middle life": Mesozoic (or "The Age of Reptiles") and "New life": Cænozoic (or "The Age of Mammals"). Each age contained fossils very different from the stage beneath it.

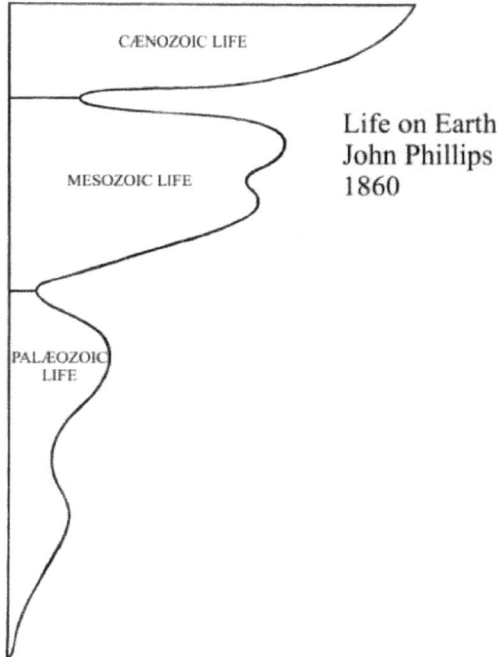

CÆNOZOIC LIFE

MESOZOIC LIFE

PALÆOZOIC LIFE

Life on Earth
John Phillips
1860

His diagram showed more and more fossils were found as you moved up through the layers. He even showed a bend in the curve mid-Paleozoic. Today we call it Romer's gap, named after paleontologist Alfred Romer, who first recognized a layer where tetrapod fossils were missing. So far, modern work still agrees with the conclusions Phillips reached.

Phillips' Image As A Tool.

So now we have a tool. Phillips' graph.
But I have to be careful.
It would be easy to slide into just telling. Telling. Telling.
I have to pay attention to where the kids are emotionally.
Who makes sense of this information?

They made hieroglyph Z-for-Zorro graphs from their own data.
The image made sense because they made it themselves. They could compare graphs with others and compare implications.

This graph is different.
The image was crafted by John Phillips.
It is interesting, but it doesn't "belong" to my students.
Yet.

I have to remember it is not the knowing of this idea that is important.
Most adults today have not learned of Phillips diagram.
What is important is that its presence allows the opportunity for discovery.
For the sudden connecting of an idea.
For the empowerment of an "aha!"

Incubation.
I have to let it sit in the "backwater" of their brains
Ready to be brought forth at unexpected times.
It is the unexpectedness that empowers. Not the memory of a
diagram.

How do I do that?
How do I build familiarity?

I sneakily prime the pump.
I have to make sure it doesn't leave their attention.
Very often a student will bring in information about the time
periods.
They are actually talking to their parents!
Families are being brought into the learning environment.
I welcome that.

There is an interplay.
Kids bring in tidbits.
I add a little detail.
They think they are generating the information as arrows collect on
the image.
Just a few minutes per day so students think *they* are constructing
the ideas.

I can tell they are having conversations about it at home. I show a
Phillips' diagram on the overhead screen and add arrows reflecting
what students have brought in. Since I teach three periods of this
subject per day, I have to be careful not to have the information
gathered and presented by one class simply told to the next class.
Rather than post the images on the wall, I project them as ideas
come up.

Students are ready for activity. They need a change in pace.

Although we seemed to have moved on to another topic, (making Astrolabes), we are actually leading in to an understanding of how we know our latitude. They busy themselves with lab activity, yet they continue to think about Phillips a few minutes per day.

Soon our diagram fills out with explanatory arrows.
What do we know about life in Phillips' Paleozoic? Mesozoic? Cenozoic?

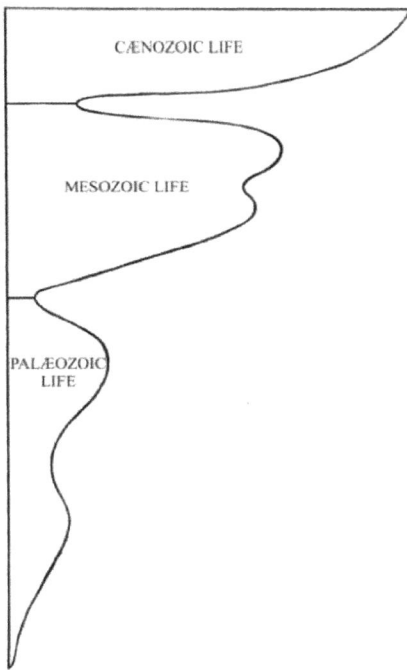

PALEOZOIC
The bottom bulge in Phillips' diagram represents fossils found in layers low on the hillside. At the beginning of the Paleozoic, life seemed to be only in or near the ocean.

Pound stones. Sea Urchins. William Smith weighed butter using Sea Urchin fossils. Where did they live? Where do they live today? Well, in many parts of the world but often in cold water.

Today Roderick Sloan collects gourmet Sea Urchins near a bleak Norwegian coastal village 88 miles north of the Arctic Circle. Why the Arctic? Wouldn't they prefer warm water? Perhaps the reason is that cold water holds substantially more oxygen than warm water does. Sea Urchins in frigid water. That seems odd.

The Cambrian explosion. Life in the sea was suddenly beginning to have shells. Trilobites, shellfish, corals, and sponges Why shells? What advantage was there in having a shell? Was it to keep from being eaten? Maybe. But paleontologist Peter Ward thinks there might have been another reason. He thinks clamshells helped channel the flow of water over their soft gills. Was the world low in oxygen? Was this a response to breathing better?

 As Trilobites got bigger they seemed to replicate parts. Bigger bodies needed more legs. And maybe more lungs. Peter Ward thinks arthropods grew repeated gill sections as a way to increase lung size 600 million years ago

Plants and animals began coming out on land. It must have been green. The Ordovician layers contain plant fossils and the Devonian layers contain fossils of forests of primitive conifers and ferns. Huge forests and swamplands formed during the warm climate of the Mississippian and Pennsylvanian periods. These became the coal beds William Smith was looking for. Animals of this time were spiders and insects and then amphibian-like and finally reptiles by the end of the Paleozoic.

Near the end of the Paleozoic, everything got big. Really big. In 1979 a dragonfly with wingspan of 20 inches was found in Bolsover, Derbyshire, in a coal seam formed in the Carboniferous time period (300 million years ago). Today Dragonflies have wingspans of about 4 inches. Other bugs were big too. Mayflies wings spanned 19 inches. Millipedes stretched 39 inches. A spider's legs spanned 18 inches. Scorpions reached a meter long. Amphibians grew 16 feet long. Ferns turned into trees. Was oxygen high? Did a high oxygen atmosphere help them grow big?

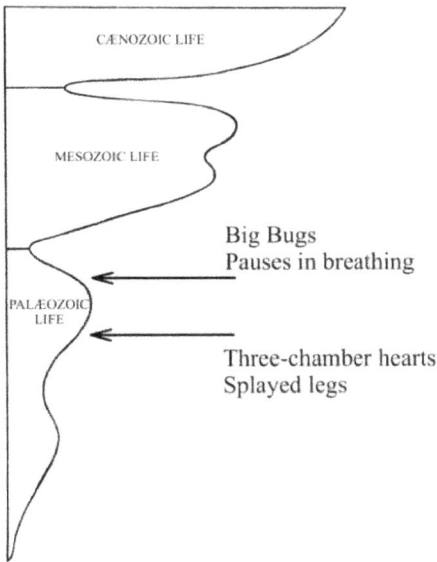

Breathing got strange near the end of the Paleozoic. Today we notice that bugs, large or small, sometimes stop breathing for a minute or two. They just pause - and then they continue on their way. Why would they do this? It is as if they collect the oxygen they need and then wait while their body uses some of it. They let their oxygen "reservoir" lower a bit before they fill it again. Do bugs get too much oxygen?

When animals came out on land in the Paleozoic, their legs were splayed out. They were sort of like fish using fins as legs. They twisted as they ran. Then, near the end of the Paleozoic, animal bodies were supported off the ground on stubby bent legs. They didn't have to drag their belly as they ran. Still, they could not breathe and run at the same time – so they were ambush predators – like the Komodo Dragon. They would chase a few feet and then stop and pant a minute. Then they would chase again.

Most reptiles have three-chambered hearts. We studied four-chambered hearts. We know a lot about them. Can we weave that knowledge base into a framework to explore three-chamber hearts? Three-chamber hearts allow some mixing of blood. Was this useful at the end of the Paleozoic? Why would you want to mix oxygenated and non-oxygenated blood? Wouldn't that reduce the amount of oxygen available to body cells? Well yes, but that might be helpful if there was too much oxygen. Oxygen is actually a poison and too much can harm us. Could a three-chamber heart provide protection from too much oxygen in the atmosphere?

So which was it? Low oxygen? High oxygen? What type of
evidence do we need to decide this?

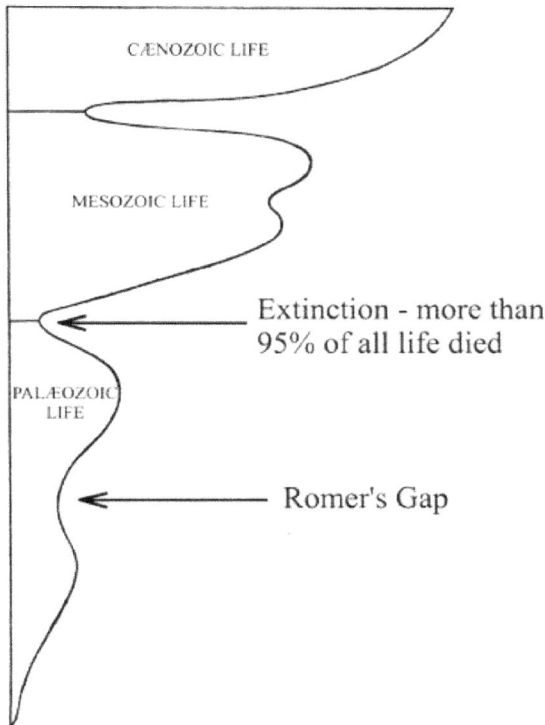

We now know the Paleozoic had several mass extinctions. John
Phillips drew the suggestion of extinction half way through the
Paleozoic. What caused them? Was it the same cause every time?
Did oxygen start low and then get higher and higher until it
crashed, killing everything adapted to the high oxygen level? Did
that happen over and over? Today we believe about 95% of all life
on Earth died at the end of the Permian. Phillips got it right!

MESOZOIC
But what happened next?
We climb up the bank and find the layer with no fossils.
Above that we find fossils again. But life was different now.

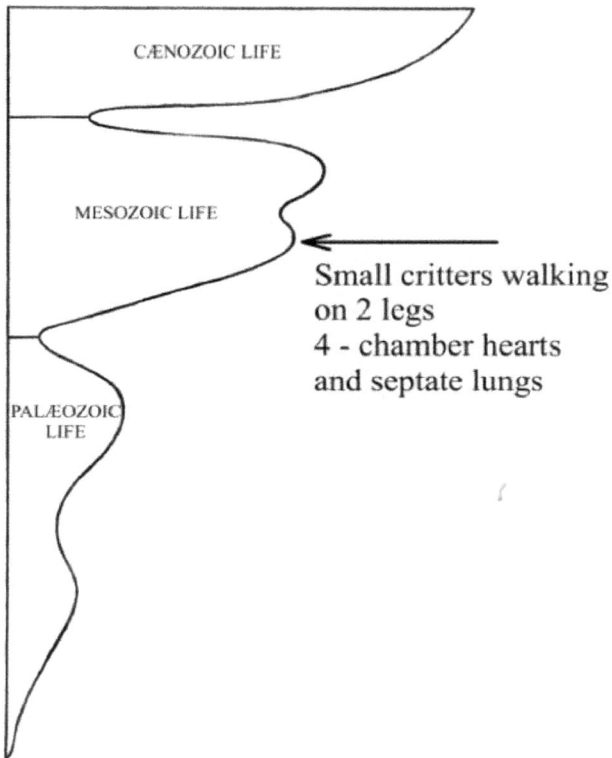

CÆNOZOIC LIFE

MESOZOIC LIFE

Small critters walking
on 2 legs
4 - chamber hearts
and septate lungs

PALÆOZOIC
LIFE

There were small critters walking on two legs. They had grown a
septum separating the ventricles. Four-chamber hearts. We call
them dinosaurs.

Many modern groups of insects such as ants, butterflies. aphids, grasshoppers, and termites were there. Birds and mammal-like reptiles arrived on the scene. And of course, dinosaurs. Large and small. Pterodactyls along with marine reptiles hunted in the seas. The first mammals were there in the form of synapsids. New plants were there. By the end of the era, huge ferns were common and the first conifers appeared. Deciduous trees and flowering plants also left fossils. It was warm and plants grew rapidly.

But warmth is not enough. Fossils at the end of the Paleozoic suggest that oxygen was low as the Mesozoic began. How did animals adjust to low oxygen? Well, they were small at first. Those three chamber hearts would not be helpful in low oxygen conditions, so what did they do? They grew a septum down the middle of the ventricles making the heart have four chambers. Now that was a good idea! A four-chambered heart sends every bit of oxygenated blood immediately on its way to nourish body cells.

Instead of dragging themselves around on splayed legs, they tucked legs under them and held their little bodies high. Most of the developing dinosaurs rose up on two legs – like little birds. Legs got longer. Now they could run and breathe. It wasn't until much later when oxygen had increased and their size got larger that dinosaurs leaned over on four legs again.

What about birds that fly high up in mountains and yet swoop low over the sea? How can they do that? High Oxygen, low Oxygen. Bird lungs are remarkable. They use oxygen in an amazingly efficient way. Rather than using alveoli they divide lung spaces with septums. Septate lungs. And air sacks. By storing air in a sack system in bones, they established counter-current flow to extract the maximum oxygen from the passing air.

The system was developed in the Mesozoic and is still used today letting birds fly high over mountains where oxygen is very low.

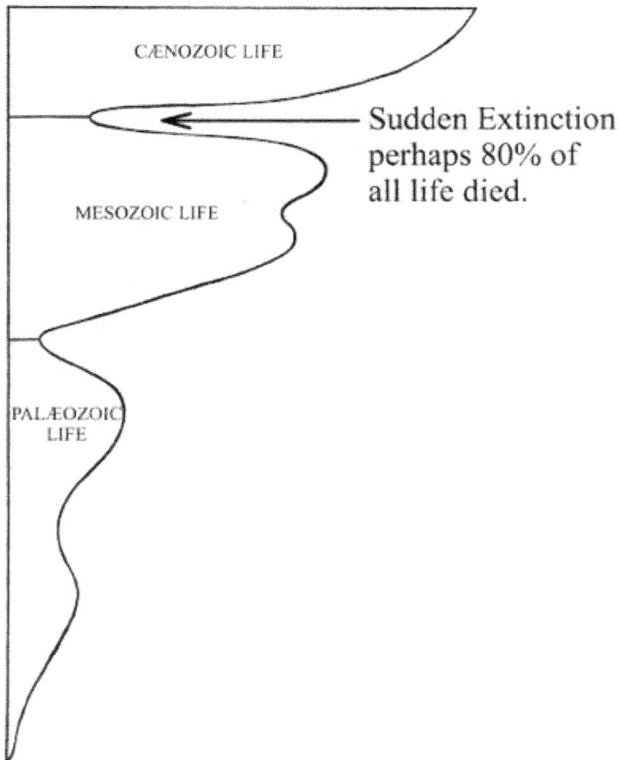

Phillips shows his Mesozoic ending suddenly. We can now give it a date: 65 million years ago. Another mass extinction like those in the Paleozoic. This was the great extinction in which the dinosaurs died out along with marine reptiles such as the ichthyosaurs, plesiosaurs, and mosasaurs. We now know that more than half of all existing life forms disappeared, including virtually all of the dinosaurs. Was the oxygen low again? Had those animals that had grown to need more oxygen, as it increased in the air, suddenly found themselves asphyxiated?

Veterinarian Cynthia Marshall Faux of the Museum of the Rockies and Yale University's Peabody Museum, and Kevin Padian, professor of integrative biology and curator of the Museum of Paleontology at the University of California, think the common dinosaur death pose showing a backward thrown head on a curved neck with jaws open is just like asphyxiated horses. The fossils certainly suggest low oxygen was the cause of death.

An ostrich-like dinosaur, *Struthiomimus*; in the classic posture indicative of brain damage and asphyxiation at death. Drawn from specimen at American Museum of Natural History. The skull is about a foot long.

http://www.berkeley.edu/news/media/releases/2007/06/06_deathth roes.shtml

Oddly enough many groups such as flowering plants, snails and clams, amphibians, lizards, snakes, crocodiles, and mammals lived through this extinction. Why? We don't really know.

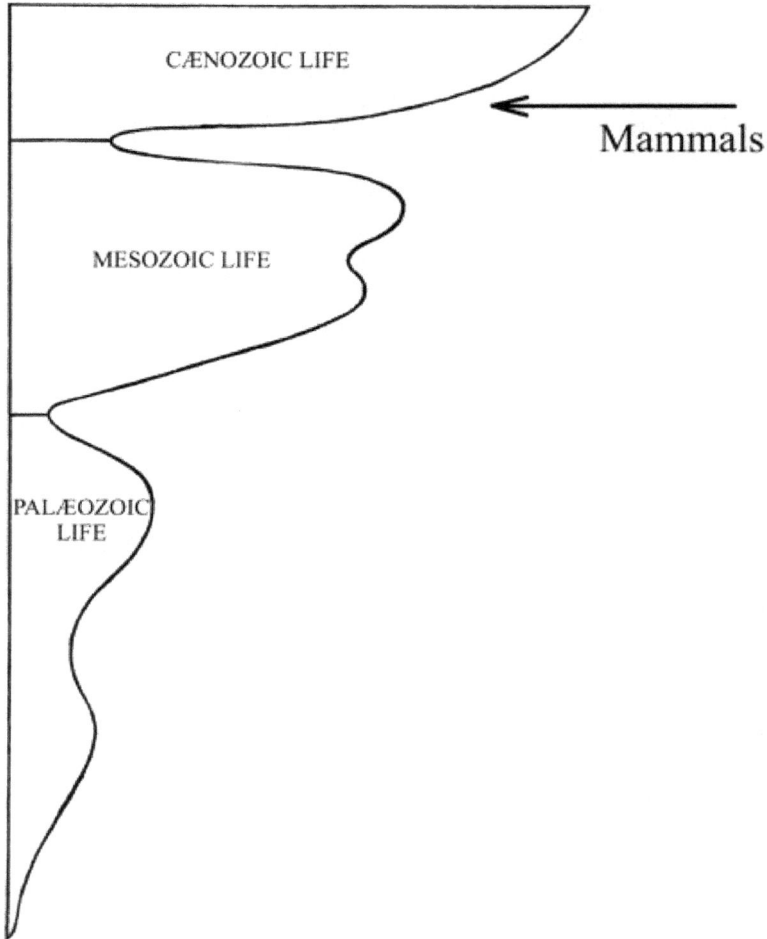

CÆNOZOIC LIFE

Mammals

MESOZOIC LIFE

PALÆOZOIC LIFE

CENOZOIC
The highest lump in John Phillips' chart is called the Cenozoic. New life. The final assemblage of life is represented by a lot of mammals. Many previous life forms are gone. No Dinosaurs! But lots and lots of different life forms.

CULTIVATING MEANING IN THE SCIENCE CLASSROOM

Mammals developed from small, mouse-like critters into giant rhinos, elephants, lions, horses and deer. Those dinosaurs that made it through the extinction became our birds. The seas filled with whales and porpoises and our wide variety of fish.

How did they do it? How did they live through low oxygen times? What adjustments in their physical form made living in low oxygen possible? Mammals already had a four-chamber heart. What other new attributes did they invent?

Reproduction changed.
Why did live-birth develop? Why mammals? There are three types of mammals: placental mammals, marsupials (such as opossums and kangaroos), and monotremes. The monotremes are warm-blooded, have hair, and produce milk just like other mammals, but they lay eggs and do not give live birth. Why? Eggs have their own problems. How could their eggs live (eat and breathe) long enough to hatch. How could they keep from drying up when laid on land? When did eggshells develop? How could the hatchling breathe inside a shell?

What about staying warm on land? Paleozoic times were cold at least at the poles. What about staying warm? Sea living allows a fairly constant temperature. In air you get hot and cold. Being a very large size retains a more constant body temperature but it also takes longer to warm up. By the end of the Permian (300 million years ago), reptiles were 12 feet long. They split into fish eaters, plant eaters and meat eaters. To help adjust their temperature, both meat eaters and plant eaters often had a large fin on their back that they raised so the morning sun would heat their blood quickly.

Not so in the Cenozoic. Suddenly there were warm-blooded critters. They stayed a constant temperature from their own metabolism.

Noses changed. Nasal turbinates are important in warm-blooded animals because they breathe so much. Outgoing breath includes a lot of water. Animals could easily lose too much water and dehydrate. Thomas Wolosz of Plattsburgh University (Nasal Turbinates and Hot Blooded Dinos) claims we breathe ten times more air per inhalation than cold-blooded animals. We need more oxygen to keep our stepped-up metabolic engineering going.

What do we know about oxygen? We notice that animals don't live on mountaintops where there is too little oxygen. Mammals nest up to 14,000'. Birds nest up to 18,000'. Birds can live at higher altitudes than similar size lizards. In the Alps most life is below 10,000. Humans get Altitude sickness above 15,000. Mt. Everest is 26,000" and has 7% oxygen in the atmosphere. Our atmosphere today is about 21% oxygen. Fifty million years ago it was higher. Many mammals were larger then. Is that a coincidence?

It Took A Hundred Years

Students are becoming familiar with John Phillips' diagram. They know that he made the image from the number of fossils in layers of the hillside. They have discussed how the image has continued to be helpful as more detail has been discovered about fossil life forms over the last hundred years.

In some instructional settings this might seem like a good time to give a test. Have students learned the material covered in class? Can I evaluate them? Can I give them a grade? Can I report their competence to parents and administrators?

Well, I could.
But why?
What is the point?
Am I interested in them knowing the diagram or am I concerned with their using the diagram for reasoning? Process or product?
Grades and judgment would destroy the magic of the dialogue.
It is not to be judged.
But, actually, children do like to know how they are doing in a class.
How to give feedback without humiliation?

Now that we have had so much discussion, so many comments brought in from home and more added by me, I can now put Phillips' image on the wall.
It has meaning for the students.
Students from all three periods see more than the image when they look at the diagram.

I can say to them, "Do you think you are ready for a test on this?"

We have a discussion to rehearse what they might put down with arrows pointing to various parts of the image.

So, the next day, I pass out blank papers and say, "Draw Phillips' diagram and label what you can."

After collecting the papers, I say, "It looks like people got quite a few arrows." "How many do you think would be a good score?"

Students suggest what might be a good number. I return the papers. I turn on the overhead projector and draw the image. We go around the room suggesting arrows and labels to be added to my sketch. I say, "Count up what you think you got." "What you were able to put down."

"Well, good for you!'
"Really?"

I collect the papers and keep them for future reference. I do not assign grades. Each student knows how well they think they did. They have feedback but they do not have me standing in judgment.

They each have some acquaintance with Phillips' diagram. At very least, they all labeled extinction events. At the inflection points there were no fossils.
No dead bodies.
No life.
Extinctions
Those are the points to focus on.
Those will provide the moments of discovery as more ideas are presented.
Individual children can learn more, but they have each absorbed the basic idea.

CULTIVATING MEANING IN THE SCIENCE CLASSROOM

It doesn't matter how much more.
I can cheer for everyone.

I am their leader, not their humiliation. Their mentor, not their judge.

The image stays on the wall.
There are more discoveries to be made.
Profound discoveries.
Moments of aha!"
But they don't know that yet.

I tape record each class I teach in order to capture their insightful comments.
We never listen to the tapes but students are proud that their comments matter.

As I have developed this lesson sequence over the past twelve years, I have discovered the connecting moments.
I can expect the "aha!"
I just have to orchestrate it well.

But, how do I do that?
These are children.
They have to be active to personalize the learning.
They have to build up a bank of experiences upon which to draw.

They have just worked on the meaning of shadows projected by an upright stick in the ground. They have worked through the logic that they can deduce their position on earth from that. Latitude. They have each constructed an Astrolabe and discussed how explorers used them to tell their location as they sailed across the earth.

Soon we will turn to a new topic. Magnetism. Geomagnetism.
"Where and what is Magnetic North?"
I ask the question on a half-page test.

Students recognize that, although they may have heard the term,
they don't know.
I plan to "set them up" to understand the clincher argument that
convinced scientists that continents moved. The magnetic-reversal
record in the rocks of the ocean floor. I can't just tell them this.
They have to understand a bit about magnets first.

OK.
Lets start with a magnet.
What is a field?
What is the shape of a field?
Can you map the field around a strong magnet using paper clips?
William Gilbert discovered the shape of the field.
William Gilbert figured out the shape of Earth's field.
Using his ideas, explorers were able to deduce where they were on
earth.

Levitate a paper clip. Tie a paperclip on a string so it floats under a
magnet.
What materials can you insert in the gap so the clip doesn't fall?

If the core of the earth is a magnet, what could the mantle be made
of?
The mantle is more-or-less invisible to earth's magnetic field.
What could the mantle be made of"

Paper doesn't stop the field.
Scissors do.
Goggles are invisible.
We play with materials as we play with the idea.

But we need to go farther.
Who is the man in this picture?
His wife won a Nobel prize.
So did he.
Pierre Curie.
He worked out our understanding of magnetism.
You have to raise the temperature of iron above the "Curie"
temperature and then cool it in a strong field.
Red-orange hot.
We can do that with dissecting pins in an alcohol burner.
Take data. Count the seconds red-hot.

Oh my goodness!
There is a photo of erupting lava on the wall! Red-orange hot!
Erupting lava is above the Curie temperature.
After eruption, rock cools in Earth's strong magnetic field.
By 1959 we had magnetometers sensitive enough to detect the
magnetic field in cooled basalt lava. You could discover the
latitude at which the rock erupted by studying the field.

But one more idea.
What is the relation between electricity and magnetism?
Orienteering compasses point to Magnetic North.
They also point to a wire connected to the ends of a battery.
Tap the wire to the battery and the compass needle moves.
With the right cadence, you can make it spin.
You can make it reverse.

Sometimes the compass needle turns clockwise, sometimes counter clockwise
In fact, Earth's magnetic field is like that. It reverses.
These ideas don't happen overnight.
They are carefully introduced and explored.
Played with over a period of weeks.
Play is vital to understanding.
Play comes before "aha."

Interspersed, we talk about the evidence we have that continents moved.
Landforms fit.
Rocks correlate between South America and Africa.
Fossils match.
Striations suggest continents clustered at the South Pole.
Large Igneous Provinces match on North America, South America and Africa.
We call the lava CAMP: Central Atlantic Magmatic Province.
We each prepare a 20 page "evidence folder" carefully setting out the arguments with data and images.

The clincher argument convincing everyone that continents move was the publication of maps of the ocean floors showing mirror-image stripes of magnetic reversals. The mirror image moved out from spreading centers.
A very cool idea.
Lets play with that.
Each lab makes a moving map out of frosting.
And they remember "Frosting Day" for years to come.

Phillips & Moving Continents

But, there is Phillips' diagram still on the wall.

Is there a relation between his layers of fossils and the moving of continents?
Well, yes.
But Phillips just deals with the last part of the timeline.

The Earth is 4.5 billion years old.
Supercontinents cycle every 300ma to 500 ma years.
That means there could have been 8 supercontinents at most.
Probably more like six or seven since Earth was hot at first.

Phillips' image just shows the last 600 ma years.
Just the period of time animals had shells.
Just when life came out on land.

Phillips' image correlates with mountains forming and continents crunching .

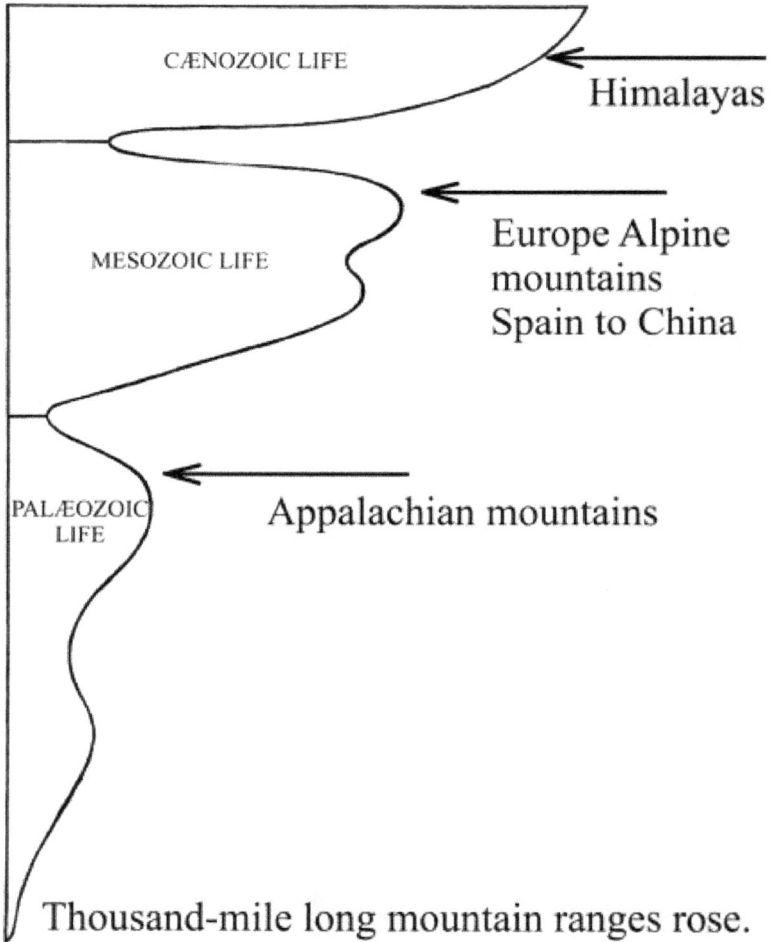

CÆNOZOIC LIFE

Himalayas

MESOZOIC LIFE

Europe Alpine
mountains
Spain to China

PALÆOZOIC
LIFE

Appalachian mountains

Thousand-mile long mountain ranges rose.

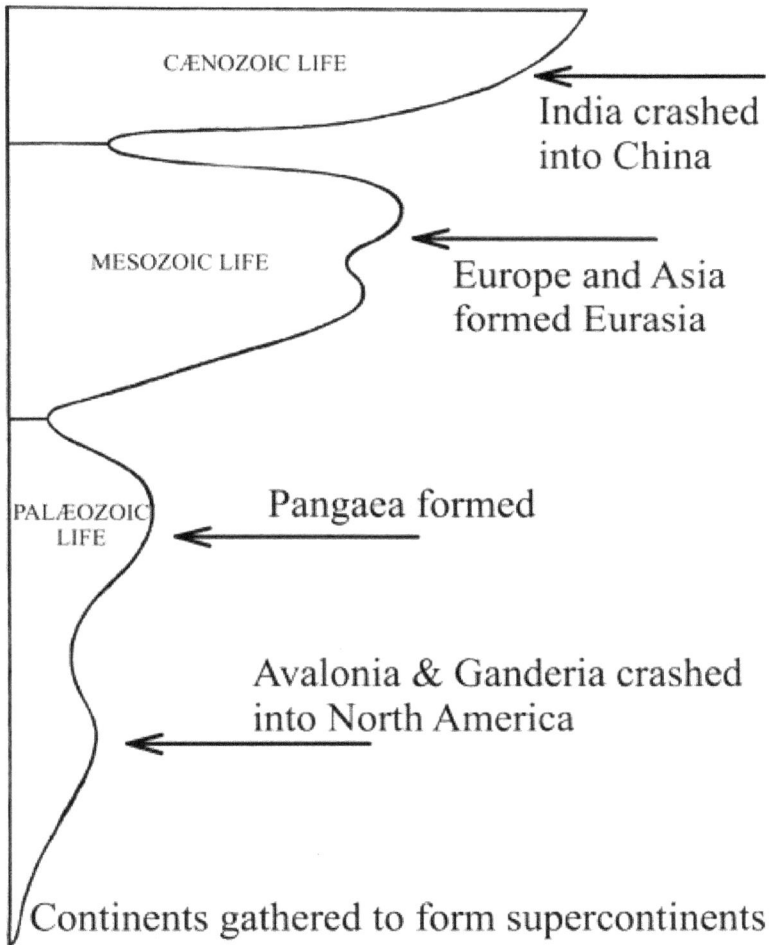

CÆNOZOIC LIFE

India crashed
into China

MESOZOIC LIFE

Europe and Asia
formed Eurasia

PALÆOZOIC
LIFE

Pangaea formed

Avalonia & Ganderia crashed
into North America

Continents gathered to form supercontinents

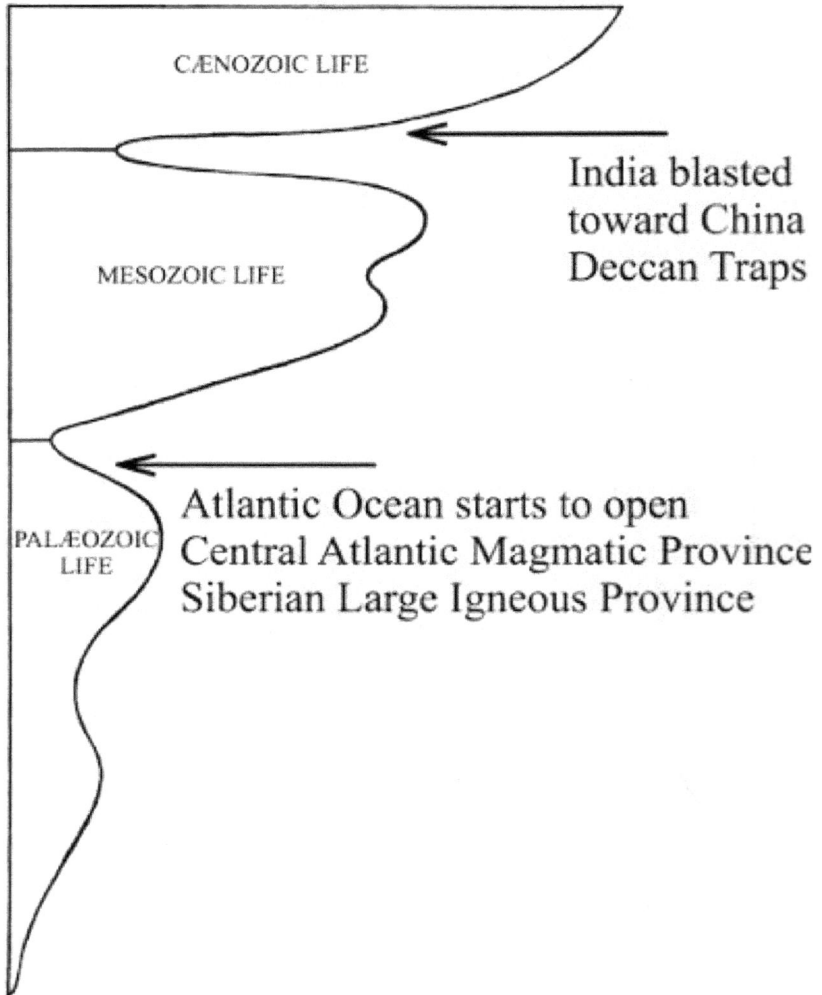

CÆNOZOIC LIFE

India blasted
toward China
Deccan Traps

MESOZOIC LIFE

Atlantic Ocean starts to open
Central Atlantic Magmatic Province
Siberian Large Igneous Province

PALÆOZOIC
LIFE

Not only that, Phillips' diagram correlates with when continents split apart with huge outflows of lava. Large Igneous Provinces.

<u>Oxygen Changes</u>

So, I watch the children.
They are enthused with their discoveries about magnetism.
They love working with batteries.
Winding coils.
Playing with reversing fields.

"Look what I can do!"
"Oh my goodness!"
"Who is our local expert?
"Can you beat that?"
Play. And compare. And compete just a little.

I watch the children.
And I watch the news.
Sooner or later a headline will scream about global warming.
Carbon Dioxide is rising!
Oh, that must be bad!

The Phillips' diagram is still on the wall.
Students ask if Phillips' image has anything to tell us about that.
Well, it might.

It is time to continue the story a little.

The Atmosphere

We have been wondering a lot about oxygen in the atmosphere. It hasn't always been the way it is today. We have about 21% oxygen in the atmosphere right now but a few million years ago it was 25%.
In the 1980's Robert Berner of Yale University began the study of the composition of earth's atmosphere over time. He first tackled Carbon Dioxide.

He published a now-famous graph. It looks like carbon dioxide spiked just then the greatest extinction happened at the end of the Paleozoic. What about Carbon dioxide would cause an extinction?

CARBON DIOXIDE GRAPH

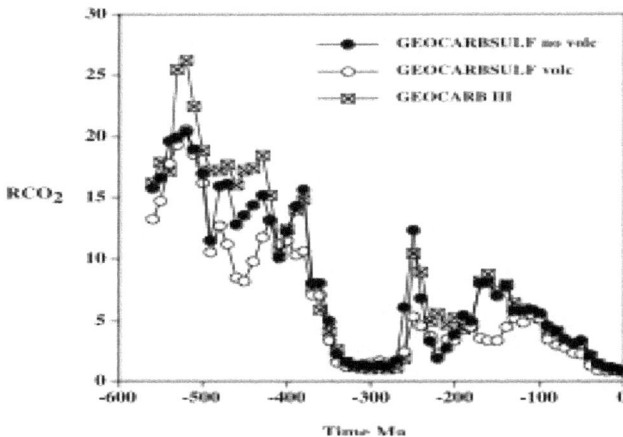

http://www.sciencedirect.com/science/article/pii/S0016703706002
031 Research was supported by Grant DE-FG02- 01ER15173 of the U.S. Department of Energy. GEOCARBSULF: A combined model for Phanerozoic atmospheric O2 and CO2. Figure 18

Well, did anything else about the atmosphere change? Berner began untangling the historic rise and fall of oxygen. He published another famous graph.

OXYGEN GRAPH

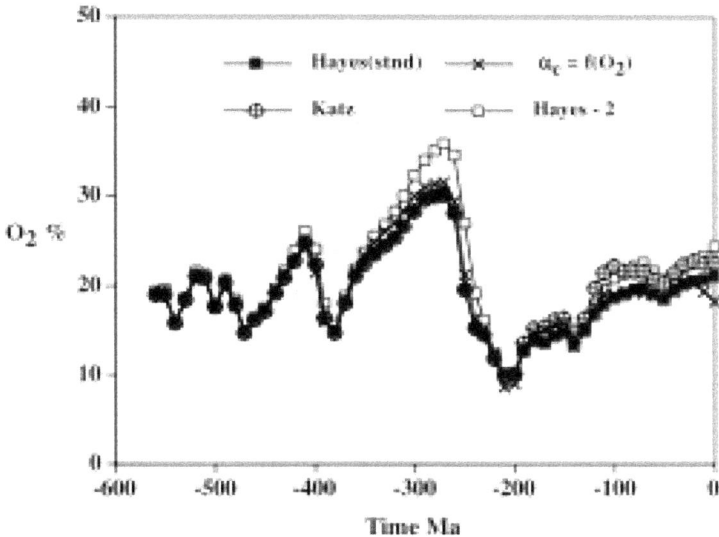

http://www.sciencedirect.com/science/article/pii/S0016703706002031 Research was supported by Grant DE-FG02- 01ER15173 of the U.S. Department of Energy. GEOCARBSULF: A combined model for Phanerozoic atmospheric O2 and CO2. Figure 13

Well, that is interesting. It looks like oxygen crashes just as carbon dioxide spikes.
How does that make sense?

OXYGEN GRAPH ABOVE THE CARBON DIOXIDE GRAPH

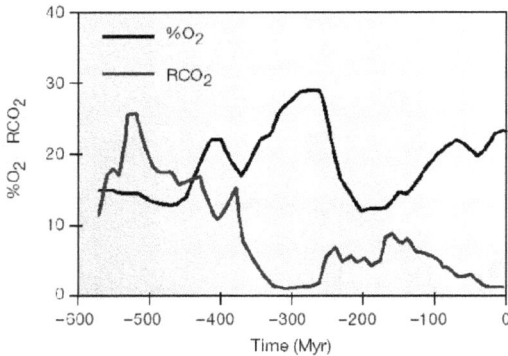

Robert A. Burner
Nature 426, 323-326 (November 2003)
Doi:10.1038/nature02131

Oh yes, the equation for photosynthesis. And the equation for burning.
They are both displayed on the wall in front of us.

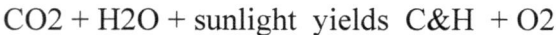

$CO_2 + H_2O$ + sunlight yields C&H + O_2

C&H + O_2 yields $CO_2 + H_2O$ + energy

It is reasonable that Carbon Dioxide would spike when Oxygen is combined.

Combining Oxygen gives off Carbon Dioxide.
We can make sense of equations by comparing the graphs.

"Wait a minute!"
A student notices something.
"Look! "Look at the Phillips' and Oxygen graphs!"
"If you turn Phillips' graph on its side it pretty much matches
Berner's oxygen graph!" "Oh my goodness!"
"Low oxygen matches extinction!"
The class is silent
Amazed.
Awestruck.
Then comments erupt.
"Oh yes, you see this, and this …"
I make transparencies and project the graphs on the overhead.
Oh my!

The graphs represent very different things, yet there seems to be
some inflection points that match. Phillips' graph shows more and
more life evolving so the "lumps" get bigger. But do the
extinctions match when Oxygen dips – even a little? How much a
change in Oxygen is necessary for life to be in trouble? Why?

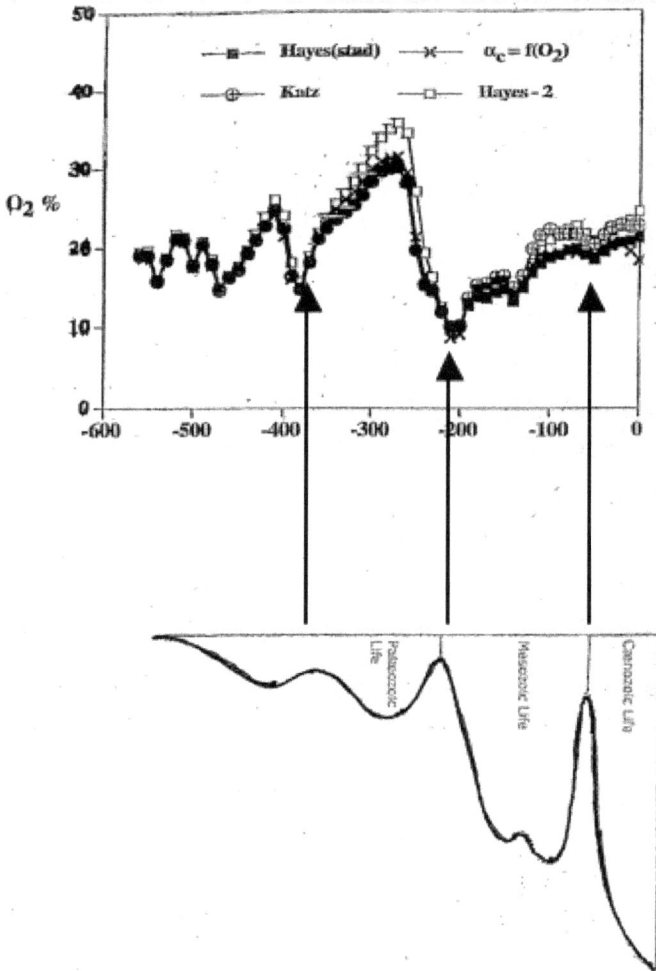

Of course! Of course.

Times of lowering oxygen should agree with times of extinction.
If you can't breathe you can't live.

It took more than a hundred and twenty years to get enough data to
correlate the graphs.
But they do match.
They seem to be saying the same thing.
There is something about the way the earth works that endures.
It is not just life forms. It is changing atmosphere too.

So,
Atmosphere changes.
Sometimes Oxygen is 35% and sometimes it is 12%.
That is a lot of change.

And life forms change.
Sometimes most of them die.
Extinctions.
Then new life forms flourish.

And continents move.
We have gathered a lot of evidence for believing that in our
evidence portfolios.

But what does that have to do with magnetism?
All of our labs recently have been related to magnetism.
What can Phillips' image say about magnetism?

Magnetism

Some students search the Internet.
Earth has a magnetic field.
It reverses.
What can be found about when and how often?
Wikipedia shows a barcode for reversals.
North points north or north points south.
Black or white.
That seems easy.

There doesn't seem to be much pattern to the flips.
Periods of a constant field are called Chrons.
Once in a while there is an extended time when the field does not flip.

Superchrons.

Someone suggests comparing it to Phillips' graph.
You never know what you might discover.

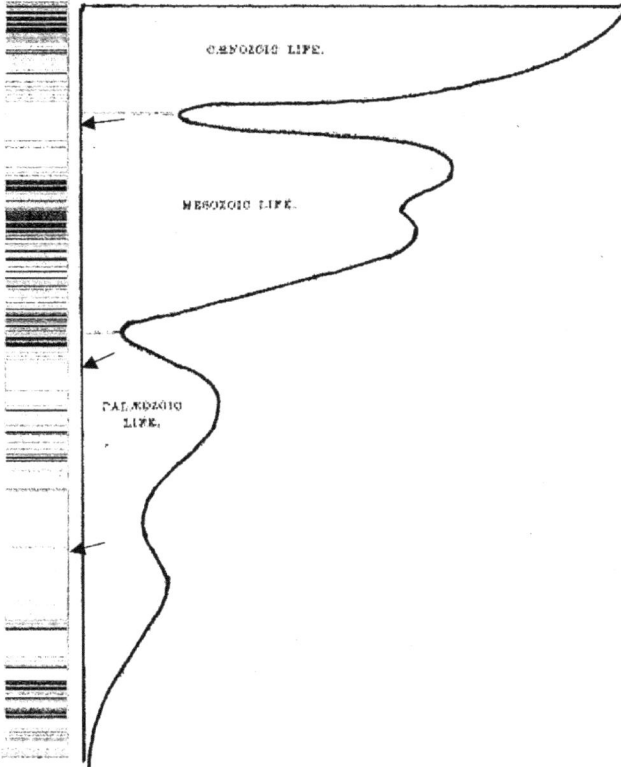

Mantle superplumes induce geomagnetic superchrons *Peter Olson [1]* and Hagay Amit*   Support for PO was provided by the National Science Foundation through Frontiers in Earth System Dynamics Grant EAR-1135382.   Portion of figure 3

More Questions

The year is drawing to a close and we have more questions than ever.

Why do Superchrons happen just before extinctions?
Why do Superchrons happen at all?
What is going on inside the earth anyway?
The core is magnetic and the mantle is not.
What happens at that boundary?
The inner core is solid. And growing all the time.
The mantle has convection cells. Up, Over. Down.
Why?
Oh my goodness?
Someone remembers Latent Heat.
As the inner core becomes solid, it has to kick out heat.
That heat must rise into the mantle.
When continents collide, they don't just disappear.
What happens to the rocks that get shoved down?
They are called Slabs.
If we were to study earth science again next year, we would want to find out about slabs. Do slabs sink through the mantle?
How does the mantle churn to produce continent motion?
Continents move across.
Slabs sink down.
What comes up?
Plumes. Mantle plumes.
What can we learn about plumes?
Plumes make outflows of lava.
Large Igneous Provinces.
They erupt from time to time.
Does their eruption correlate with Phillips' diagram?

We have a lot more to learn.
The way the earth heat engine works is certainly interesting!
Especially if we discover it for ourselves.

www.ingramcontent.com/pod-product-compliance
Lightning Source LLC
Chambersburg PA
CBHW072044040426
42447CB00012BB/3007